REPUTATION DRIVEN

TOP REAL ESTATE PROFESSIONALS REVEAL WHY HAVING A GREAT REPUTATION IS THE BEST MILLION DOLLAR BRANDING STRATEGY

AMA PUBLISHING

CONTENTS

FOREWORD

As I sat across the room from him, I couldn't help but notice how anxious and hopeless he looked. He was so anxious, that I could see that his hands were trembling along with his voice!

He began telling me his story, and I could tell that he was on the verge of tears. This was his first time meeting someone like me, yet he was willing to share his deepest, darkest insecurities. With his voice cracking, he said to me, *"I know exactly what to say to prospects on the phone, but I'm so afraid of rejection that I would avoid calling prospects altogether!"*

When I heard this, I felt a knot in my stomach because I knew what it feels like to be so afraid of rejection, that you begin to self-sabotage! That is the worst feeling to have because inevitably, you end up failing because you are focused on the "thoughts" of failing rather than the steps you should be taking!

This is a harsh reality for many individuals in the entrepreneurial and business space, especially when it comes to real estate! In 2018, *The National Association of Realtors* posted a magazine article titled "Is Real Estate a Depressing Career" on their website. In this article, they posted a study that suggested that the real estate industry was the second highest-rated profession for clinically diagnosed depression.

But that doesn't have to be you! There are *three secrets* that if unlocked will change how you approach this book, your profession, and even your life! I've seen my clients save businesses, careers, and even lives with these secrets and I'm going to share them with you. These are the mental secrets to start building a great reputation in the marketplace!

Secret #1: "You are NOT the voice inside your head."

The inner critic is a voice that we all share and the origins of it go beyond the scope of this book. However, the inner critic has one job, and it may surprise you. Its number one job is to protect you! Whenever you go outside of your comfort zone, your mind will say things like "I can't do this" or "I'm not good enough." It's your minds way of keeping you safe, and it does a great job.

So how can you overcome your inner critic so that you can make a lot of money, help to impact others, and build a strong reputation? You must begin developing an identity outside of your inner critic. If you don't, the results, as I showed earlier, can be devastating to your career and personal life! You now may be wondering "How do I do this?" Well, you could go to my website and pay me your hard-earned money, but I'm a very generous man so I'll share it with you now!

Secret #2: Start noticing your thoughts with a sense of curiosity.

Before you believe the next negative thought that your inner critic tells you, ask yourself this question: "If I allow this thought to be my leader, will it lead me to my dreams or to my doom?" If the answer is the latter, then you should speak back to your inner critic by saying something like "No, thank you" or "I got this, I appreciate it." You could simply do this in your head or even silently out loud. This technique is simple yet powerful because it will help you to separate the real *"YOU"* from the inner critic, thus freeing you from its grasp!

I want you to imagine what you could accomplish in your real estate career if you were not anxious or controlled by your inner critic. Would you post more content on social media promoting your business?

Would you follow up more with warm leads? Would you speak with more confidence when meeting with a potential buyer? The possibilities of what you can achieve are endless or as Jim Kwik says, "limitless."

Throughout your real estate journey, you will have some highlights and some lowlights. My favorite quote of all time is from Michael Jordan, who said "I've missed more than 9,000 shots in my career.... I've failed over and repeatedly in my life. And that is why I succeed." This is a common theme behind all successful individuals. They can embrace their failures without losing enthusiasm.

Therefore, real estate professionals must have a new relationship with their anxieties, failures, and even their inner critic. Those who are successful did not avoid failure. They accepted it (and themselves) while staying committed to their journey. This leads me to my final secret that will help you approach this book, real estate, and your personal life with a bulletproof mindset.

Secret #3: Confidence is not the absence of fear or failure but an acceptance of fear or failure.

What messages have you heard when it comes to fear? What messages have you heard when it comes to failure? That it's bad? You're weak if you experience it? You can't be successful if you've failed before? These are messages that I received as well about fear and failure. As a result, I did everything I could to avoid them. However, there was one problem: I was also avoiding the actions that could take me closer to my dreams.

To prove this, I want you to write down your Top Three fears or failures when it comes to real estate. Then I want you to set a timer for three minutes to imagine what your life would look like if these fears no longer held you back. If your failures didn't stop you from pursuing your dreams. Do this now!

Now, set your timer again for three minutes and write down what you saw for yourself. Do this now before moving on. Take a moment to reflect on what you imagined for yourself and then compare it to the three fears or failures that you wrote down. Now, here's the million-dollar question that I want you to ask yourself: *"Is it okay for me to feel fear or experience failure, in order to have my dream lifestyle?"* If the answer is yes, then the fears you have are worth feeling. The failures you are experiencing are worth going through. This is a simple three-step framework that you can use when you are feeling stuck due to fear or failure!

For those of you who decided to skip this exercise, did your inner critic get in the way? Did your mind say, "I'll do it later" or "I don't really have to do this." If you are wondering if I'm calling you out, then yes, you are correct (but with good intentions).

Much of this book is about the "Stories" of being reputation driven and how having a solid reputation in real estate will require you to face your fears. However, it really comes down to your application of the book, which truly makes the difference. So, as you read this book, be on the lookout for your inner critic. They will tell you "This can't work for me" simply because it wants to protect you.

In all, my hope is that you take these three secrets with you as you begin your journey throughout this book and as you read these stories. I've personally seen how it has transformed my life and I know that it will transform yours as well.

As I wrap up this foreword, I want to share with you a quick quote from Jim Kwik. He speaks of "The 7 Lies of Learning" from his book called *Limitless* and lie Number Four is "Knowledge is Power." Yes, you read that correctly. Knowledge is not power, but the application of knowledge is true power!

I've given you *three secrets* to help you shift your mindset before reading the stories in this book. You are about to take a deep dive into the knowledge of being *Reputation Driven* and what you do with it will determine if it is powerful or not.

There are two types of people in this world. You have the dabblers who read books like this, to feel smart but never take any action with it (my guess is that their inner critic wants to keep them safe). Then you have the doers. These are the people who read books like this, apply the information they've gathered, and take the real estate industry by storm. Who you decide to be after reading this book is up to YOU. You will hear about the journey of real estate professionals that decided to become doers, and I have no doubt that you will DO the same.

Until next time, my friend!

- Phillip Wells (AKA: The Players Coach)
Licensed Psychotherapist, Professional Life Coach

P.S. Robert Greene, the author of *The 48 Laws of Power* states "Do not leave your reputation to chance or gossip; it is your life's artwork, and you must craft it, hone it, and display it with the care of an artist."

Sources:

Cited: National Associations of Realtors
Cited: Robert Greene, "The 48 Laws of Power"
Cited: Jim Kwik, "Limitless"

Linktree: *www.linktr.ee/theplayerscoachllc*

PREFACE

It took hard work and dedication for me and my business partner Chris Barrett to grow our brand marketing agency for vacation rentals and real estate professionals to over six figures. And we're excited to grow to reach seven-eight figures!

We grew this business at our own pace, and we've done the hard work to build our brand in a very tight niche market. We learned how to identify our target audience based on their psychographics, target audience, and being able to put together a solid team that works remotely but feels like we're all working in the same office.

We learned to properly design and SEO optimize beautiful direct booking websites for vacation rentals and company branded websites for real estate agents and investors, and how to get our clients the results they are looking for, but there was also a problem... people still didn't know who we were, and we weren't closing clients as effectively as we should.

Just when we felt we were doing great things charging $1,800 for custom website designs and $99 per month for our Launch Plan, we noticed we weren't getting and closing enough new clients effectively. Yes, they were coming through the door, but not at the pace we wanted once we decided to press the gas on our marketing strategies.

It was depressing because we felt like we were doing awesome work for our clients. We truly loved them and cared about their results. We built close bonds with many of our clients and were happy with our performance and their outcomes.

This was great because *we would get referral clients* but struggled getting new clients. And when we did get the opportunity to speak with a new qualified prospect, it was hard to convert. Why? Because they had never heard of us, so the trust wasn't there.

One afternoon I was meeting with a past client and friend, Jodie Stirling of Stirling Stays, and she mentioned she was putting together a multi-author book called *Hospitable Hosts* and wanted our company, bnb AMPLIFY, to be part of the project by becoming a sponsor.

It was such a great idea and was hard to say no to! There would be no other book on the market like *Hospitable Hosts* and I knew this would be a great opportunity to gain more visibility and get new clients through the door.

"I really want you to be a part of this. You guys have helped me out so much that it only makes sense that you are part of this book project," said Jodie.

At the time I was aware that our closing rate was not looking good but didn't want to pay too much attention to it. Jodie truly made me think of the endless possibilities of being a part of the book project.

We didn't have much time for putting together our own YouTube videos, podcasts, and growing our Facebook group for client attraction and acquisition because we were tied down building our frameworks, systems, and processes and nurturing existing clients.

How could we really scale our business if we are struggling to get and close new clients?

What could we do to get more people noticing us with instant credibility and authority?

As I researched this further, I learned that the average non-fiction book sells about 500 copies. That's not a very impressive number if you're looking to sell books like Robert Kiyosaki, the author of *Rich Dad Poor Dad*.

For entrepreneurs, the power with becoming a published author is *not* solely about the number of books you're selling, but *most* importantly, what *exactly* your book can do for your business!

There was a survey conducted on entrepreneur-authors by Grammar Factory and it reported that...

34% of the surveyed entrepreneurs doubled their earnings since publishing their book.

63% reported being featured in online magazines,

43% in newspapers,

and 33% featured on the radio and 10% with TV appearances.

Additionally, other streams of income were opened for these surveyed entrepreneurs in the form of paid speaking engagements with 72% getting speaking gigs because of being a published author, with 33% being paid to speak at industry related events.

What about establishing strategic partnerships?

The leveraging of a book can be a great revenue booster for any real estate professional and only adds to their overall reputation assets. These surveyed entrepreneurs were also able to use their books to secure strategic partnerships beyond what running online ads could do.

74% were able to find new referral partners,

46% got distribution partners,

26% partnered with major brands in their related industries.

So, can real estate professionals grow their business by being published authors?

Yes!

In fact, 86% of the surveyed entrepreneurs reported that since becoming a published author they were able to grow their business beyond what they were doing before releasing their book.

From this point I knew we needed to make another pivot in our business to bring greater value to our clients. I analyzed the success of entrepreneurs who become authors and looked at our current service offerings and knew we needed to marry the two.

Our company, bnb AMPLIFY, will become a hybrid branding agency with a deep focus on media and publishing services for the real estate industry.

After the successful release of *Hospitable Hosts*, I reached out to Adriana Monique Alvarez at AMA Publishing and thanked her for the opportunity to help serve as a sponsor and hoped that our company could do a multi-author book for real estate professionals in the future... and this is how the *Reputation Driven* book was born.

Now that we can help our clients and real estate professionals build arguably the greatest reputation asset for their business and career, we identified these four benefits for becoming a published author as a real estate professional.

By doing this book project, these same four benefits helped our business reach a wider audience, forge strategic partnerships with the Reputation Driven authors, and raised our total sales of the book project to $48,500+ and will help to enroll future multi-author book titles that we decide to publish for the real estate industry.

When we decided to publish *Reputation Driven* and invited professionals to share their stories, and these amazing people said YES... we knew we were on to something great!

How to Gain Market Share with a Book (or a Chapter)?

We made the pivot and added a new book publishing service that will help real estate professionals gain more market share by building great reputation assets. Here are the four main benefits that we have identified for being an author: Grow Your Brand

Attraction – when you write a book, this is the best way to align your mission and purpose with your book goals, timing, and profits for the best results.

Alignment – writing, publishing, and marketing your book can better serve and attract your perfect clients, customers, and/or guests for predicted future growth.

Authority – your book will position you are the leading "go-to" expert in your industry and local area/region. It will separate you from your competitors and create raving fans.

Impact – create a great brand experience and provide a consistent brand message that resonates and elevates your readers into a raving fan base. You will change their lives!

So, I can tell you from my experience that building a solid brand comes with having reputation assets and being a published author is one of the best reputation assets you can have. Before there were websites, there were books. Before there were Facebook Ads, there were books. Having a solo book or being part of a multi-author project will not only make you more money and more successful, but it will provide predictable growth and make your business a lot more fun.

In this book, you'll read the motivational and inspirational stories of real estate professionals, and you can implement their tips and strategies to build a great reputation for yourself and business.

Now, let's go to work...

INTRODUCTION

While there are hundreds of YouTube training videos focused on "building a brand" so that you can "get" new clients, nobody tells the truth:

If you don't have credibility, visibility, and authority—then you don't have a brand.

And this is a major concern because...

64% of women and 68% of men have felt an emotional connection with a brand.

So, how do you build this type of loyalty?

Believe it or not, it's not just about online reviews.

You have probably experienced this yourself, and often asked

"why do I like this company so much?"

Well, building a solid brand and attracting your target audience comes down to what we call our "Trifecta Growth Framework," and you must dedicate yourself to the process...

If you are reading this book, chances are you are frustrated (like I was) with the difficulty of getting new clients because you don't have a brand and reputation built yet.

Maybe you've not had the luxury of building out your reputation assets to bring life to your business. Perhaps you've not learned HOW to do that, and it's one of the biggest factors holding back your real estate or vacation rental business so that you can enjoy the lifestyle that you know you deserve.

In this book, you'll get real-world experiences of true real estate professionals in the trenches. And in my chapter, I will reveal the step-by-step process we use to help our clients build solid reputation assets that deliver results.

Reputation is consistency and staying true to your craft. This leads to trust building and people recognizing your achievements over time. I say this because I want you to know that you can trust me and the stories in this book.

Since the launch of bnb AMPLIFY, I have learned many things about myself and made many good friends along the way. And for me to be recognized and awarded as one of the *Top 100 Marketing & Advertising Leaders* for 2020 because of my dedication and commitment to digital marketing, I am forever grateful. The award committee based their selection on the following:

1. Overall Reach
2. Industry Impact
3. Spirit of Innovation
4. Future Readiness
5. Market Demand

For the award committee to see my contribution to the digital marketing space over the past decade, I was extremely honored and felt it was well deserved. I have worked very hard over the past years, and nobody knows that more than my family and business partner, Chris Barrett (you'll read his chapter next).

I am proud of the branding impact we bring to the real estate and vacation rental markets through knowledge, wisdom, and understanding.

Knowledge – of our marketing systems, processes, and frameworks.

Wisdom – being able to translate those systems and frameworks to provide results.

Understanding – knowing the needs of our target audience through our Avatar Framework.

I share that personal accomplishment with you because I truly believe in what we do and know how to help you achieve success. It's in my DNA to be a problem solver and solutions provider.

On our website, we describe our *Local Brand Growth Formula* in detail. Here I will outline the following four marketing systems that you can use in your real estate business today to help you establish a strong reputation in your local market.

1. *Launch* – This is the reputation phase of the formula and requires your love and attention to detail. Here is where you will establish your reputation by developing key reputation assets to help position your brand in your local market. These assets include your website, local SEO, visual brand identity, multi-author, or solo book, etc.

2. *Nurture* – This is the referral and repeat phase because this is where you can create communication and brand positioning through automation campaigns that help establish you as the go-to expert. In this phase, you focus on referral and repeat business by building birthday campaigns, activating an old list, setting up your newsletter, etc.

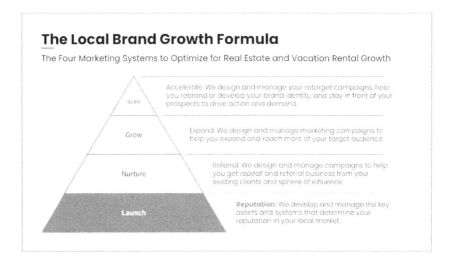

The Local Brand Growth Formula

The Four Marketing Systems to Optimize for Real Estate and Vacation Rental Growth

Scale — Accelerate: We design and manage your *retarget* campaigns, help you rebrand or develop your brand identity, and stay in front of your prospects to drive action and demand.

Grow — Expand: We design and manage marketing campaigns to help you expand and *reach* more of your target audience.

Nurture — Referral: We design and manage campaigns to help you get *repeat* and referral business from your existing clients and sphere of influence.

Launch — **Reputation:** We develop and manage the key assets and systems that determine your *reputation* in your local market.

3. Grow – Now, it's time for you to focus on *Expanding* your business so that you can reach more of your target audience. You should have invested in a powerful CRM with many capabilities that will help you create email drip campaigns, appointment booking or sales funnels, backend workflow automation, social media automation, etc.

4. Scale – Great job building your online and offline reputation and making a name for yourself. You have a website and visual brand identity and you're ready for the next level. It's time to *Accelerate* your brand! Here you'll focus on team building, sales, and other strategies like content marketing, giveaways and challenges, video marketing, reputation management, brand development, etc.

Where is your business as it relates to the four marketing systems above? How can you implement one or two of these systems into your business today?

When you are building your reputation, you can't only focus on reviews. Many real estate agents and vacation rental hosts fall into this trap!

Your reputation is more than your reviews. Your reputation is what your brand presence feels and looks like in the marketplace. And to do this successfully you must focus on your key assets and systems that will ultimately determine your reputation.

In fact, all your favorite Mega Brands follow these four marketing systems that I've described above, which we help our clients implement into their business framework.

Let's look at two mega brands that you are very familiar with, Zillow and Airbnb. These two companies are incorporating all four of these marketing systems without question!

Some clients that we speak with may have one or two of these systems in operation, but many do not. They do not pay attention to these four marketing systems which are vital.

The sad truth is...

Many real estate professionals and small business owners are implementing *none* of these marketing systems simultaneously.

For these core marketing systems to work you must *gradually* grow into them where these systems are fully integrated into your business framework. The speed at which you grow into these four systems is entirely up to you.

However, grow at your own pace... and risk!

Because the risk of growing too fast can have a negative impact on your reputation and predicted growth of revenue. When you can grow slowly and trust the process you can find the bottlenecks in your business and fix them more efficiently and effectively.

Yes, growth is what will fuel your brand for a period, but retention is what will keep your real estate business thriving and always top of mind in the eyes of your clients, customers, and guests.

1 JUDAH SWAGERTY

MY STORY

Although I am now running a successful hybrid brand marketing agency for real estate professionals, it has not been an easy ride!

My brother DiMingo and I were raised by a single mom who was also an entrepreneur! I watched her overcome so many hurdles during her journey.

She sold T-shirts and other apparel on street corners and in flea markets. She eventually opened her own storefront with my grandmother in the downtown area of her hometown.

This was such a great accomplishment for her, and I was happy to see her shine. This is what she taught me... to never give up on yourself. And to stop dreaming and start "doing" because God is always in control.

I started my first internet company in 2000, an online travel directory. I became affiliate partners with various online travel companies like Expedia, Travelocity, and many more and sold cruise packages, rental cars, and airline tickets all via my affiliate links.

I did that for about a year and had some success as I would receive checks in the mail for a few hundred dollars for vacations, rental cars, and other things that were being booked through my affiliate links.

It was from this early experience that I found my love for digital marketing. I knew that it worked, and I had proven the concept by building the affiliate site from a WYSIWYG website platform.

September 11, 2001, the entire world changed. The Twin Towers were hit by planes, and the United States was under terrorist attack. All travel would be shut down as the entire world stops.

Travel demand reduced by 31% within four months following the attacks, and it was at this time I decided to make a shift to the online travel directory. I added many more departments such as dating, employment, and business.

Me and Evelyse in Charlotte NC.

With the help of two friends, Brandon Tate and Chris Martin, we launched JKSE, an online directory that would "try" to rival Yahoo, MSN, and the new kid on the block, Google.

We built the site to over 500 pages of online access to thousands of companies that were listed within our database. Over 1,000 people used our branded email service (much like Gmail), and we are hitting 80k-100k visitors per month to our website.

There was a way to monetize all that traffic, but we didn't know how! The site was getting too big to manage and we didn't have a solid business model, so we had to shut it down.

My wife, Evelyse, just gave birth to our firstborn child not too long before we decided to shut down JKSE in 2003. I needed to take a break from the internet world and focus on something that I could touch, rather than a keyboard and mouse.

Evelyse and I went on to have five children together and decided to homeschool them because we knew that we wanted to teach a different concept than public schools. I cherished the thought of starting businesses with my children and establishing generational wealth goals with them, and I have been fortunate enough to do just that.

The COVID pandemic brought many challenges for us all. It was during this time I lost my mother and grandmother, and it shook my world forever. I now live to inspire others like they have inspired me.

The stories in this book will motivate you to take control of your life and honor your name and legacy. You now hold the tool in your hand to help you build a great reputation and serve others with integrity.

ABOUT JUDAH SWAGERTY

Judah Swagerty is a brand strategist, real estate entrepreneur, and the co-founder and visionary at bnb AMPLIFY, a hybrid brand marketing agency that helps real estate professionals and vacation rental owners launch and grow their businesses using their *Local Brand Growth Formula*, publishing and media services, and marketing automation strategies.

He has been named *Top 100 Marketing & Advertising Leaders* for 2020 and has over twenty years of experience in digital marketing, specializing in brand marketing, content strategies, and website design, and has dozens of highly successful campaigns and projects under his belt.

Judah loves helping his clients identify their target audience and build systems and frameworks, along with the right reputation assets to produce results. As a real estate entrepreneur, Judah has also devoted his time to serving others through creative real estate financing strategies and is now looking to grow a multi-family investment portfolio.

Get live training, tips, and strategies on how to implement the Local Brand Growth Formula into your real estate business. Join the *Real Estate Professionals Community* Facebook group today.

Visit me: *www.linktr.ee/judahswagerty*

2 CHRIS BARRETT

I was working part-time at a mechanic shop in a high-traffic area where motorists could get their cars washed, buy tires, and get general repairs done.

So I got to know the customers well and observed what kind of people they were, their motivations for doing business with us, and how they made decisions.

This information helped me develop my sales approach as I went from customer to customer, talking about the benefits of services, the importance of maintaining their cars, and how we could help them save money over the vehicle's lifetime. It was a simple task, but I learned a lot.

The owner was a first-time business owner who decided to have a streamlined flow of repair work in his shop he focused on improving the visual appeal of the building so that it looked nice, inviting, and professional.

His objective was to create a friendlier and more professional atmosphere for motorists and he even put up signs, a lounge area with a TV, and client seating.

In addition, he bought nifty uniforms for himself and the rest of the crew...

And eventually, motorists started stopping by for general repairs, tires, and car washes.

But one thing he should have accounted for was the tools he would need to complete jobs efficiently and effectively, which held up the workflow...

At this very moment, he had a choice: *Get the necessary tools to complete assignments at a reasonable pace or stick to what he had and try to work faster.*

Some entrepreneurs (not all) surprisingly choose to stick with the latter.

In some cases, it works for them, but in this situation, the owner chose the latter, and it did not play out well because he essentially was cutting corners.

Without the proper tools, it ultimately dampened the workflow. And to add insult to injury, the shop started getting bad reviews.

His business reputation was in jeopardy...

When faced with a problem, he didn't care to solve it. Instead, he began blaming his staff for why he was receiving bad reviews.

He was afraid to face reality...

Instead, he went out looking for a scapegoat to blame for his problem.

...And he found it.

But the solution could have been more effective. Instead, he made matters worse.

So what could have been done differently?

He could have taken the feedback as an opportunity to learn. Instead, he chose to blame his staff for his situation. In the end, his business reputation was ruined.

I later transitioned into another opportunity, but what I learned from my mechanic shop experience taught me a valuable lesson:

Building a solid reputation doesn't mean "fake it 'til you make it."

The truth is, in today's digital world, you can't fake your way to the top; people see through your tricks and lies and know who you are right down to your name.

If you want to be successful and build a name for yourself, you better be ready to work hard and make something real, not just throw together a bunch of online accounts and pretend to be someone else.

Reputation Is KING

The reputation of a business has become an equally important factor in making decisions as its financial health.

A well-established brand in the market has gained trust and credibility among customers. So it becomes a point of consideration for consumers as they select products and services.

However, it is not only financial health that matters when establishing a brand reputation; it is also the quality of products and services offered by a business. With the growing customer demands, brand names are being redefined to reflect the needs of their consumers.

In light of these changing times, it becomes essential for businesses to understand their brand reputation.

Reputation is the new king and it's one of the most powerful tools in business, both online and offline. So how can you use it to your advantage?

It would help if you built your reputation asset (website). When people search Google for your company name, products, and services, your website should come up first.

So how do you get to the top?

Focus on your reputation management...

Make sure your content is updated often. And when you have a blog, add posts that answer questions, show your audience how to solve problems, answer reviews, and keep them updated with the latest news.

Remember, reputation is about building trust and credibility. And once 'it's built, 'it's never lost.

Our brand marketing and web design agency, bnb AMPLIFY, have successfully built reputation assets for our clients and provided results time and time again. This is done through creative solutions that deliver a memorable user experience and effective website design that supports brand identity and objectives.

I am a proud brand builder, and our business is continuously evolving. I have gained experience and knowledge in this area over the years and continue learning and growing.

My core values have remained the same, but I will continue to adapt and evolve in my approach. '

I've worked hard to build a business focused on helping real estate professionals build brands that create long-term value for themselves and their clients. And it is a passion of mine to help the industry.

It takes time, patience, and persistence. You have to focus on making sure people know who you are.

This is not a get-rich-quick scheme! Building a great reputation takes time and is a life-long process.

You see...

When you become a real estate professional, you want to be surrounded by like-minded people, which can be very isolating if you're starting.

So, I've attended local real estate meet-ups and connected with like-minded individuals on social media. But you know what's great about this simple method?

Those you connect with are all going through the same thing—so you can learn from their experiences. I also read books about financial, real estate, business, and personal development. If you're interested in growing your money, you must immerse yourself in the topic.

It takes time, but you can build a community of friends with the right people. Remember not to be afraid to ask questions when meeting someone new. You might not know precisely what they do, but you can still make them feel welcome by asking about their company and goals.

What I'm Doing, What I'm Working On Now, and How I'm Planning To Get There

What I'm doing in my business is taking what I have, learning from it, and making sure I'm using it to its full potential, so I'm not reinventing the wheel. Instead, I continue to operate and improve on the things I learned in my other businesses. The truth is, I have a cheat code to create systems and use the things I've learned from previous experiences to get my job done.

I am currently actively looking for properties to purchase but have also been active in the market to increase my overall value as a professional. While I would love to continue purchasing real estate, my focus is now on improving my overall market value.

This means I've been networking with other industry professionals and genuine people and actively working on my professional branding and marketing strategies. I am also starting to target the STR/MTR (short-term/mid-term) rental market for my first rental property.

I love creating, and I am working on lots of different projects. If you like to follow my journey, I would love for you to stay up to date with me and all my future endeavors.

 "Your network is your net worth."

JIM ROHN

Remember that story about the mechanic earlier in this chapter?

The tools were not only one of the prominent components of his setback; it was the relationship between his staff and himself. When he did not take accountability for his actions and shifted the blame to his team, he inevitably failed to fix the actual problem.

As a leader, you must be prepared to shoulder the blame for your failures. If you do not accept full responsibility for your actions and their outcomes, you are sending a message to your staff that their hard work does not matter.

What he could have done better was create an environment that promotes fairness, ultimately creating ambassadors for his shop.

However, the fact remains that if the business treats its employees fairly, the word will spread, and it will receive positive feedback from the community. The same applies to the customers—the public will embrace and appreciate the brand if they're treated well. This is a sure way to have an excellent reputation in the marketplace.

The best news?

If you are reading this, you are already on an excellent start to becoming reputation driven. You can begin building your reputation today! Most people dive head first in endeavors but never take account of people who are tried and true veterans, and in this book, you will be able to hear firsthand experiences from many of the great authors in the chapters ahead.

So don't wait another minute—Stay engaged... ONWARD!

ABOUT CHRIS BARRETT

Chris Barrett is a brand strategist and real estate entrepreneur with a focus on wholesaling and other creative financing strategies. He is also the co-founder at bnb AMPLIFY who helps real estate agents, investors, property managers, and short-term rental hosts solve problems and scale their businesses with marketing systems, automation software, and creating reputation assets while building a local brand. He is highly respected in his community as a father, online thought leader, and businessman who knows the power of being Reputation Driven. After reading his story, you will quickly learn why having a great reputation is the best million-dollar branding strategy for your business or career.

Visit me: *www.linktr.ee/bnbAMPLIFY*

3 ANDREW HANSON

My Sincere Thanks to Judah Swagerty for getting me involved in this publication. May it lead everyone involved to great achievements.
To all my fellow Hospitable Hosts Authors joining us in this publication: what an honor to do it all again with you! Huge thanks to all the collaborating RD Authors for making this publication a reality!
With a special thanks to my wonderful wife, mom, dad, nephews, niece and entire family, friends, HH Authors, AMA Publishing and all our tremendous vendors for their support of all my business endeavors.
Again, I'm beyond thrilled to be part of this book and to share my story, especially because books have been a huge part of my success and mentorship over the years!

As the title of the book suggests, reputation is extremely important in business and all other endeavors in life. I believe a person's reputation is shaped by their character, ethics, and morals. Throughout my journey in real estate and business, my character has helped open doors for me that I couldn't have opened otherwise. For those readers who are familiar with commercial lending, "Character" is part of the 5 Cs of Credit, which is important to any real estate investor's success. Character is crucial to reputation, and I will be sharing testimonials that speak to my own character. These testimonials highlight my continued drive to succeed and provide examples as to why I believe actions and character lead to an impeccable reputation. I would suggest that everyone driven to succeed collect letters of recommendation as well as testimonials throughout their career. In addition to providing a strong testament to the character and reputation of their company, they also can help remind those driven to succeed just how far they have come and how far their reputation has driven them.

"Be more concerned with your character than your reputation, because your character is what you really are, while your reputation is merely what others think you are."

JOHN WOODEN

"Character is like a tree and reputation like a shadow. The shadow is what we think of it; the tree is the real thing."

ABRAHAM LINCOLN

"Attend well to your character and your reputation will look out for itself."

NAPOLEON HILL

Here's a little bit about my Driven Story!

My name is Andrew Hanson. I am thirty-eight years old at the time of writing this chapter. I'm entrepreneurial and extremely passionate about all things real estate: investing, banking, hospitality, small business and most recently my newfound passion for writing and teaching others about financial freedom and investing in real estate. My wife's name is Meghan, and we live in a small rural town in the beautiful Lake Sunapee Region of New Hampshire in the United States of America. New Hampshire is a vacationer's paradise, with all four seasons packed full of recreation activity and an abundance of outdoor space, wildlife and state parks to enjoy. Tourism and small business in New Hampshire are a large part of our local economy and a very important revenue stream for the state and its residents.

Meghan and I both come from humble family backgrounds and grew up in lower-income families. Tragically, when Meghan was seventeen, she lost her dad to suicide. A few years later, when we were in our 20s, we decided to move to New Hampshire from Massachusetts. We were young and ready for a new start together. We looked toward New Hampshire and its tremendous wildlife, year-round outdoor recreation activities, large lake regions, and the free-spirited lifestyle of the New Hampshire citizens. So, after a little searching, we purchased our first house and started out on our new life together. We had no family in the area; only one friend in the area. We had no jobs, and had only $3,000 in our savings account. We took a chance at a new beginning for our lives in New Hampshire and are very glad that we did! Meghan and I have been extremely private with our journey, struggles and personal lives, we have recently discovered that sharing our story of breaking down barriers, working hard and never giving up can show other couples that it doesn't matter what you background is if you dream big and work hard you can rise to the top while also help serve others in your community!

Photo taken by Tiffany Hall, a great friend.

Building a Reputation of hard work at an entry level!

I found an entry-level job as a maintenance technician. I was truly fortunate to be working with experienced techs overseeing anywhere from around 1,500 to 1,800 rental units, everything from over fifty-five senior housing, large multi-family complexes, student housing, commercial real estate, industrial spaces and high-quality vacation homes in the Vermont and New Hampshire mountains. Having many years in this role as a hands-on certified maintenance technician was excellent exposure for me. I was able to learn at a young age the inner workings of maintenance operations, property management in a wide variety of sectors, maintaining and protecting assets, and the relationship between proper facility maintenance and being successful at owning real estate assets. After many years as a hands-on technician working in the field every day, I worked my way up to become a hands-on property manager of a 144-unit condominium complex in my local community. From there with a great support team of employees that supported me and trusted my leadership, I soon progressed to a property manager of several complexes throughout the state. In total, I was managing over 350 rental units, a $38 million portfolio, in the state of New Hampshire. My wife Meghan had similar professional progress—she landed an entry-level job at a local bank starting out in their file room. During her sixteen-year tenure at the bank, she held various roles from Loan Servicer, Senior Commercial Loan Assistant and Assistant Vice President Commercial Workout Officer. Meghan is proud of her years of professional banking experience, and she applies her underwriting, risk mitigation management and commercial banking skills to our real estate companies and to the benefit of our clients and collaborators. Meghan also is proud to apply her years of commercial banking insights by currently volunteering on a board of directors for a local non-profit credit union that proudly serves over 18,000 members in our local community.

At the age of twenty-eight, I was honored to be recognized as the 2012 Young Professional of the Year by the Claremont Chamber of Commerce. I have also been fortunate to serve as a director on several non-profit boards in my community, allowing me to continually give back to the community I fell in love with as a young man. More recently, because of my reputation and philanthropy over the years, I am honored to say I currently serve as a volunteer on the supervisory committee for a local nonprofit credit union that is proudly serving over 18,000 members, serving both states of Vermont and New Hampshire's communities. I have also recently studied to earn the Certified Credit Union Supervisory Committee Member (CCUSC) Designation the gold standard designation in the industry. I also hold several real estate management certificates from the Institute of Real Estate Management. I am also an EPA/HUD RRP Certified Lead Renovator. I'm very proud of the RRP and Lead Abatement work CITYSCAPE LLC, I and the staff have completed over the last five years in our community. It's a great feeling to know that we have helped successfully remove lead orders and helped properly remediate many properties throughout our community, making housing safer for families that reside in them. The one thing in life that I am most proud of is having years of hands-on remodeling and construction experience working with my dad when I was growing up. I am also thankful for all my dad's hands-on construction help when I first started out in real estate. It is an amazing trait and passion we both have been able to share together throughout the years of working hands-on together on so many properties and construction projects.

It was an Honor to receive this in a formal letter from a US Senator when I was 28 years old:

"Congratulations for being recognized as the greater Clare-mont Chamber of Commerce Young Professional of the Year. The commitment you've shown to the community has had a positive impact on the lives that you touch. I appreciate all that you do to help create jobs, stimulate our economy and make New Hampshire such a special place in which to live, work, and raise a family."

KELLY A., US SENATOR, NEW HAMPSHIRE.

The Driven Desire for financial and time freedom!

In 2011, when I was still working as a property manager for W-2 income, I had a strong desire burning in me to become financially free for my family's future. That strong desire, combined with my reputation as a successful property manager, community-driven leader and my deep passion for real estate, helped me start CITYSCAPE LLC on the side with a truly great friend and partner. At the time, we started the company as a simple investment company that was buying and holding a few real estate assets for cashflow while also providing around two fix and flip transactions every year. I am happy to say that the original vision has evolved into far more over the years. In 2015, I bought out my business partner and became the sole owner of the company. Fast forward to 2022 and we have turned into CS companies, a family of specialized companies in the real estate industry. Our family of companies now owns and operates many real estate holding companies, each with their own organizational structure and unique missions. All our companies operate in different sectors of the real estate industry. On top of the Real Estate holding companies, I still own and operate CITYSCAPE LLC, a real estate development company that provides a variety of specialty services in the real estate service industry. Our specialty is providing property preservation, stabilization and REO services to financial institutions, realtors, and investors. In 2020, Meghan and I started Pond Life Vacation Rentals, a vacation rental management company providing high-quality vacation rental experiences to our guests. Our family of companies have built reputations of their own, building off our original character and reputation in the industries we have served over the past twelve years.

I share with you two different letters of recommendation I have received, one from a long-time client/vendor and one from a former employee that worked for me for many years:

Letter of Recommendation from a client:

> I write this letter of recommendation for Andrew Hanson CEO of CITYSCAPE LLC and his affiliates companies.
>
> Through the years of working with Andrew I have had a chance to get to know him as a person, I have found him to be an extremely hard working, motivated, professional person as well as business owner. This hard work and motivation have led Andrew to compile his own very impressive real estate portfolio spanning several area towns, both residential and commercial real estate.
>
> Andrew's experience with his own properties, as well as through his business is extensive and impressive. I would not hesitate to recommend his company as a top notch, well rounded real estate service company.
>
> Justin Ranney,
> Owner/Broker Coldwell Banker Homes Unlimited

Letter of Recommendation from an employee:

> I have never seen anyone that continually puts such enthusiasm and passion into their work. Andrew also brings that same passion and enthusiasm when volunteering to better his community. He is well liked and respected.
>
> Successful property management requires a unique individual that can think on his feet, deal with anything at a moment's notice, all while handing ten other things.

Andrew Hanson is that type of individual. He exudes confidence and leadership and has a special talent for making those of us that work with him feel that we are not only necessary, but special, and that all of our hard work is appreciated. I am so proud to have worked for him.

Cherie R.,
Property Manager

My most recent Driven Journey as a "Hospitable Host"

Meghan and I have always had a love for all things real estate investing and traveling, but I never knew how much I would end up enjoying the hospitality side of the portfolio. In 2020, after years in other sectors of real estate, at a time when we were faced with great adversity in our lives, we decided to start a new venture in the short-term rental space.

We were already in the rental business for years; we had an Airbnb account already set up in 2018 for personal travel. At this time, one of our properties already had a furnished studio apartment we rented to traveling nurses for years, and we had several waterfront and water access rentals. These properties seemed ideal for starting our first venture into this market. This decision started our journey to becoming hospitable hosts.

In July 2020, Meghan and I founded Pond Life Vacation Rentals. Pond Life Vacation Rentals is a real estate vacation rental management company providing families access to all of New Hampshire's outdoor activities. Although started the company right as the COVID-19 pandemic was ramping up and many had concerns about the strength of this part of the real estate industry, we continued to push forward with our vision. There were many skeptics. Often, I received words of caution from those that thought vacation rentals were nightmares to manage. I'm very happy to say that we persevered through the trying times of the pandemic knowing that we have provided people from all walks of life with an opportunity to reconnect with nature and have access to water and outdoor environments. This was our WHY and we uphold these values to this day.

Pond Life Vacation Rentals has performed extremely well since its inception. We are finding that guests have rediscovered a desire to be with nature. Pond Life Vacation Rentals offers vacation rentals to all income levels and all walks of life. We have had the honor to host top corporate CEOs, farmers, local travelers, those looking to move to New Hampshire, and many more at our properties. It's a great feeling to be in the position to provide these guests with a peaceful sanctuary, either for their short-term vacation or temporary stay needs. We get to see and meet all kinds of people from all walks of life and they often share their stories about why they're traveling. We are proud to have built a company reputation for creating memory-making experiences for our guests to cherish for years to come. On top of that Meghan, has also built a cleaning division that has garnered a great reputation for five-star STR cleaning, helping support other hosts in the Lake Sunapee area while also landing several high-net-worth clients for our service company.

Pond Life Vacation Rentals has been an amazing experience for me on a personal level as well as a professional one. It was created out of hardship that popped up and require me to pivot a bit, but my character, perseverance, family support and reputation drove me out of adversity and forward towards our mission. That adversity planted a seed of greatness in my life, a seed that blossomed even further when I was contacted by Jodie Stirling about becoming an author in Hospitable Hosts. The personal call was amazing, and she was incredibly supportive of me joining the book. I was honored to be presented with the opportunity, especially after spending many nights listening to many of the hosts talk on Clubhouse. Oftentimes on my journey as a business owner, I listen to audiobooks on self-improvement and developing a productive mindset. I did the same with Clubhouse, listening to and applying the advice the hosts were giving. I listened every Sunday like clockwork to the other authors. I am proud to be a part of the *Hospitable Hosts* book and to know the other amazing authors involved in it. To anyone who has not picked up a copy, I would recommend buying it. It has crucial information for anyone interested in the STR and vacation rental industry. It's available on Amazon, and I'm on chapter 25. There will also be a Volume 2 released in 2023 with more great industry professionals.

Here's a review from a recent guest:

> We love it here! We'll continue to come back time and time again as the beauty is surreal! The hosts are awesome people! Thanks for a wonderful place to stay during our 4th of July weekend!
>
> Jauntessa "The Little Cabin Retreat" Croydon, NH on July 4, 2022

Testimonial from a Short-Term Rental cleaning client

> We used Cityscape for the first time this year for our short-term rental turnover cleaning. I can't rave enough about their services: Every time the house was meticulously clean, and the crew always showed up and was on time by the minute. Meghan is simply a pleasure to work with. She is very responsive (even on weekends and holidays) and she thinks along the whole time trying to make life easy for her clients. Can't recommend their services enough if you have high standards and want peace of mind.
>
> Pascale,
> Vacation Rental Homeowner - Sunapee, NH

Here's a recent review from a guest:

It's difficult to meet our standards for cleanliness, but this place surpassed them. The location was perfect for accessing Dartmouth, the mountains, and the lakes. And you really can't find a safer location.

Joey H.
"The Studio at 57 Main" Newport NH October, 2022

SunSetter Cabin

Driven for collaborative relationships with others!

We are always seeking opportunities to collaborate on deals and acquire real estate assets. Our flexible entrepreneurial spirit allows us to react quickly to evaluate opportunities and potential management partnerships. Our full-service real estate development company can provide a broad range of services to our clients, including consulting on purchasing, full remodeling, construction, property preservation, maintenance and help with consulting on values for selling rental properties to other investors in the marketplace.

I personally also offer select coaching, business mentoring, and consulting to select like-minded individuals looking for professional advice for their businesses to help propel and advise them in the real estate industry. By signing up for one of my monthly mastermind or yearly couples real estate wealth and health retreats, you will get me as that motivational mentor to help guide you through the ups and downs of the business and real estate industry.

I'll leave you with one last testimonial that means a lot to me personally. It's from a boss I had when I was still starting out in real estate. I was fortunate to have worked for him and his family. They exposed me to the ideas of generational wealth and the velocity of money. His family supported my personal growth, showed me through what they accomplished that I could achieve anything, and taught me how important it is to have a strong character and reputation in the industry you serve.

Testimonial from my prior employer when I was still working for a W-2 as a property manager:

> It has been inspiring to have Andrew as the Manager and Overseer of all 3 complexes.
> Over the years as our Manager Andrew has presented himself as a person of honesty and integrity. Most of his staff are older than him. They look up to him for his leadership, and truly find pleasure in working for him. Because of his personal qualities, his intelligence, and his work ethic he is left on his own most of the time to Manage multimillion complexes.
> On a personal level I have a great deal of respect

for Andrew. He is a leader and person that other young people can look up to for inspiration. Andrew came from very little and in that way, he demonstrates that this is the land of the free. He has gone out and worked hard showing that you can pull yourself up no matter what your background is and rise to the top.

Chris Thomas,
DLC Investments, New Hampshire

My Driven Desire to share, educate and motivate others

I have found a deep desire to share my knowledge with others and encourage them on their path to financial and time freedom. Books have been a large part of my success. When I was in my early 20s, a great friend and business partner handed me *Rich Dad Poor Dad* by Robert T Kiyosaki. That book, followed by many others in the *Rich Dad Advisors* series, along with so many other countless books, has helped shape my outlook and allowed me to have a mindset of abundance as an entrepreneur and small business owner. I cannot suggest enough how important reading and learning are to one's self-improvement. For people on the move, as I usually am, audiobooks are a great option. I have relied heavily on audiobooks and still do to this day. I enjoy teaching others the benefit of real estate investing, cashflow, and the velocity of money. I have seen firsthand the long-lasting financial freedom and generational wealth it can create and my family is fortunate to be on the path of financial and time freedom. Recently, I have started on my newest book publication called "The Property Maintenance Playbook: What every investor and property manager need to know to succeed in the real estate industry." I hope to educate these owners so they can apply the six principles of property maintenance that have helped me succeed, and I want to help those owners adapt those principles to their rental portfolios. This book is to help simplify life for you as an investor or property manager. You can order the book from my linktree account *www.linktr.ee/AndrewHanson* or contact my office directly to purchase and get directly shipped a signed copy of the book.

A reputation for building common ground relations with others

I have found that building relationships with others while also finding a way to serve others is key to helping with the balance of being in harmony with the laws of nature. Building mutually beneficial relationships has helped me help strike a balance throughout my career. Balancing your existing relationships and creating new ones with potential vendors, city officials, employees, clients and tenants can be a juggling act for many business owners as it has been at times for me. I believe as you go through your journey of life, you will be met with many obstacles and problems but if you stay strong, honest and hold true to your character you will have the willingness to adapt, change and survive. There is success behind being able to adapt while making changes to your context or reality. Changing your reality of perspective will lead you to always find solutions. You should also beware you may be met many times in life with people who naturally are critics, bullies, cynics, disbelievers, pessimists, worriers, and many people that will just make assumptions without any facts of the matter. There will be many who will try to discourage you from your desires, visions and dreams. My advice is to stay the course even during times of temporary defeat. Most of the time, you can still find common ground with mutual benefits for all involved in matters that are presented with resistance from others.

 If the thing you wish to do is right, and you believe in it, go ahead and do it! Put your dream across, and never mind what 'they' say if you meet with temporary defeat, for 'they', perhaps, do not know that every failure brings with it the seed of an equivalent success.

NAPOLEON HILL, THINK AND GROW RICH

ABOUT ANDREW HANSON

Andrew is a performance-driven, multi-faceted, strategic real estate professional with a twenty-year track record of leading complex real estate projects, investments and construction to optimize ROI and exponentially grow sales. He leverages and shares expertise in all areas of real estate to facilitate significant and sustainable revenue growth. Andrew's experience, coming from a low-income family, gave him a great appreciation and compassion for his employees, residents and guests. His experience in construction, as a child who worked with his father remodeling properties, gave him a boots-on-the-ground perspective he applies to the projects he oversees. Since 2011, Andrew has owned CS Companies, a family of specialized real estate companies. Their main goal is to oversee, organize and thrust affiliates' missions forward with the highest level of integrity. At age twenty-eight, Andrew was recognized as the 2012 Young Professional of the Year by the Claremont Chamber of Commerce. He holds several real estate management accreditations from IREM and is an EPA/HUD RRP Certified Lead Renovator. In 2020, Andrew moved into the short-term rental space and co-founded Pond Life Vacation Rentals, through which he provides memorable vacation experiences at his amazing properties. Andrew also serves as a Supervisory Committee Member on a Non-Profit Credit Union and he holds the CCUSC designation from CUNA which is the industry Gold Standard Designation. Andrew spends his spare time in nature and on the water, boating and floating with his wonderful wife, family, friends and French bulldog.

Linktr.ee: www.linktr.ee/AndrewHanson

4 MARK SIMPSON

Most people's journey into holiday rentals or short-term rentals is by accident. They fall into it via Real Estate or investing in property.

I was born into it.

On a 200-acre farm just off the Yorkshire Coastline in a seaside resort called Scarborough.

A little known fact is that Scarborough is the second most visited tourist location in the UK after London.

Every other house seems to be a bed-and-breakfast, hotel, or holiday rental.

My parents transformed their 200-acre farm in the late 80s when farming declined. My dad never went to school and can barely spell, but he and my mum had the guts, determination, and work ethic to give it a go.

No analytical tools or software in the 80s gave you insights on Return on Investment.

It was sheer belief and hard work.

And then I came along.

Growing up, people always surrounded me.

It was customary to always have a stranger in my house.

At night, I was paraded in front of our guests, enjoying an evening meal to say good night to everyone.

As I got older, I would help set the same room for breakfast before jumping on the school bus.

My school holidays were filled with making new friends every day as guests from all over the UK, and then later years the world, would come to stay.

My parent's farm stay business was one of the first in the county and was a huge success.

At the turn of the decade, they knocked down a barn and added on more rooms to make it fourteen in total.

Added in a cafe and restaurant and went all in on the hospitality business.

The main driver of the business was repeat guests and word of mouth.

Remember, this was a time without the internet, Airbnb, or social media.

It was newspaper and magazine ads and people talking about their stay to their friends, co-workers, and family.

It was a reputation-driven business.

And one that would eventually sell for seven figures.

However, this chapter is about a specific tactic that I discovered that you could implement into your business straight away.

This tactic costs nothing.

This tactic is simple to do.

This tactic works in any industry or business, and anyone reading this can use it.

Before I tell you this, do me one favour and send me a message on Instagram to let me know you're reading this book.

I have published several best-selling books on Amazon now, so when you send me a message, let me know you're reading the reputation book.

If you're an STR or Vacation Rental host and you have an Airbnb listing and would like me to take a look at it, send the link over. I would love to check it out and see where you could make some amendments to boost your profits and turn more Lookers into Bookers.

My Instagram handle is @boostlyuk

The step-by-step guide on how to become the go-to in your location and niche.

I love marketing. I love to break down how things work.

When a guest used to book with us at our farm stay business, I would start to survey them to find out.

- How they found our business,
- Why they booked with us,
- What they were coming to the area for.

I wouldn't just take the generic answer of "I found you on Google."

I wanted to delve down to specifics:

- What made us stand out,
- Which picture caught your attention,
- Is there an event or special occasion in the area that you're coming to,
- Is it work or pleasure?

You will be surprised at how many people were up for helping and answering the questions.

I would ask via email after they had booked (sometimes called them) or when they arrived on the property.

As a marketer, it was everything I needed to know.

It helped me to delve deeper into certain tactics that we were doing and stop focusing on the ones that weren't.

In 2015, there was a big shift in the online space.

Instant bookings were becoming more of a thing.

Cell phones were getting more powerful and easier to use and with this the guest booking process was changing.

Booking.com aka The Booking Holidays Group, The Expedia Group, and a little plucky wasb was starting to take up the majority of the top spots on Google search and the public were gravitating more to their websites.

We started to see a rise in bookings via the OTAs (Online Travel Agents) and with that our profits were decreasing as we were having to pay more in commission costs.

Also, I noticed that the types of guests we were getting weren't the types we wanted on the farm.

When a booking comes in from an OTA, they send anyone.

It wasn't sustainable, and we had plans to scale and eventually sell our business and retire my parents.

I went back to what I know best: surveying our guests.

This time, I started to ask different questions.

ASK BETTER QUESTIONS

This time I was asking the questions during their stay or after their stay.

"When you stayed with us, where did you go and visit?"

"Which local businesses did you visit?"

The reason for doing this was to compile a list of places, whether it be restaurants, pubs, markets, attractions or day trips of local businesses for our future guests.

It was to enhance their guest experience and to create a local itinerary before they arrive.

The outcome was to not only increase our direct bookings, cut down on our OTA bookings, boost our profits and more importantly increase the local word of mouth about our business and heighten our reputation not only locally but in our niche too.

From surveying our guests, I discovered that there were three locally owned businesses that our guests were visiting 80% of the time.

I Googled their business, got the email and phone number, and reached out to the owner.

I explained that we had a thousand guests visit us every year, and we were sending them to their business. *FOR FREE.*

Which business owner would not love to hear that?

I asked if there could be any discount or coupon for our guests so we could recommend more people to go to their business, which they duly obliged.

I went into the conversation with...

How can I help you and not expect anything in return?

We basically created a WIN, WIN.

WIN for our guests as they had a recommended place to visit where we knew they would have a good time and also had a discount code exclusive to them because they were staying with us on the farm.

WIN for the business owner of the local attraction who was getting more customers for zero ad spend and zero work.

And the ultimate WIN came for us later down the line.

WIN #1 - My family and I never had to pay when we went to the attraction on a day off.

WIN #2 - the business in question started to offer weddings at their venue. It was trendy. They didn't offer accommodation, and when the bride and groom would ask for where the owner recommended for their guests to stay, where do you think they mentioned?

Now, the business owner of the attraction didn't tell us, but one day our phone and emails started to go crazy.

People called saying they were getting married at the attraction, and they needed a place to stay.

The best thing about wedding guests is that they book way in advance.

We had money in the bank and calendar dates sorted for a year, eighteen months in advance.

We had to open our calendars for twenty-four months ahead of time, which was unheard of before.

The proof in the model was there.

I went to more local businesses and adopted similar relationships and partnerships with them.

I marketed our services and accommodation to more *local* businesses.

99% of the other accommodation businesses wouldn't dream of marketing to local people or companies, because they were thinking too short sighted and only marketing to people out of town.

When everyone was zigging, I was zagging.

And the results spoke for themselves.

Even with the growth of Airbnb, we used them as a marketing channel. That's it.

We didn't care about an algorithm change on their search.

We didn't notice when Facebook made it harder for businesses to be organically found.

We double-dived down on taking that offline word of mouth online. We worked with local businesses to create partnerships and relationships that would last for years to come before we eventually sold the company for seven figures and retired my parents.

During that time, I created the *Hospitality Community Facebook group* (come and find it), and I started to document what I was doing at our farm stay business to help other hosts get better educated on how to market their business and not over-rely on third parties to generate their bookings.

Every day I was posting help and guidance and tips.

Hosts were jumping into my inbox and asking questions.

I spent more time answering hosts' questions than emailing guests, so I created a podcast and blog; you may have heard of it.

The Boostly Podcast

Seven years later, it is in the top 1% of downloads in the whole of the podcasting world, and Boostly is the go-to direct bookings website design agency and training company worldwide.

Come and say hi on Instagram via @boostlyuk.

Thank you for reading this chapter.

I hope you have picked up a few "a-ha" moments that you can bring into your business.

Whether it is real estate, short-term rentals, or anything else you're doing to generate financial freedom.

The underlying message from my chapter and the whole book will present to you is that if you try to go this alone and not create relationships, friendships, and partnerships, it will take you much longer to achieve your goals.

Your Network is your Net Worth

We are now firmly in the sharing economy.

So take advantage of it and go and increase your network.

ABOUT MARK SIMPSON

Following an epic career in all realms of hospitality, Mark has worked with thousands of short-stay accommodation owners to date, helping them skyrocket their direct bookings.

Established in 2016, Boostly is now a globally recognised leader in hospitality marketing and gives hosts the tools, tactics, and training to boost their profits—with actionable advice.

Staying true to his life's motto, "Done is better than perfect," what makes Mark a leader of the pack is his consistency, proactivity, and commendable ability to "show up" whenever (and wherever!) necessary.

Mark is on a mission to help one million hosts and property management companies reduce their over-reliance on Airbnb and VRBO.

You can keep in touch with Mark via Instagram *@boostlyuk*, and check out his best-selling books, *The Book Direct Playbook* and *The Book Direct Blueprint,* on Amazon.

Website: *www.boostly.co.uk/website*
Instagram: *www.instagram.com/boostlyuk*

5 PAM HOLT

I t's 1985, and home mortgage interest rates are 14%. Walter Payton and the Chicago Bears would finish their season with a fifteen to one record, and then go on to win the Super Bowl. Michael Jordan would injure his ankle in his third game with the Bulls and end up sitting out for sixty-four games that season. Chicago, my hometown, topped the list as one of the most segregated cities in the world.

It was also the year I decided to become a real estate agent.

After graduating from college with a BS in Architecture, Design, and Urban Planning, I took a gig as an art director for a major advertising agency. Although I enjoyed the work, I knew I wanted to be in control of how much income I would earn and at the same time explore my passion for residential architecture. Obtaining my real estate license seemed like the best way to accomplish both goals, so I went to work selling homes in Chicago's central neighborhoods.

What I didn't realize was that I would be the only African-American agent working in those neighborhoods.

Chicago is a city of seventy-eight unique and diverse neighborhoods. Back then, those neighborhoods were—and sadly still are—largely divided. The traditional Black and Brown neighborhoods are on the south and west sides. The lakefront, the downtown, and the neighborhoods around the lakefront remain mostly White.

For real estate agents, the north-south dividing line was Congress Parkway—now known as Ida B. Wells Drive in honor of the African-American investigative journalist, educator, and co-founder of the National Association for the Advancement of Colored People.

This division was clearly represented by the fact that the multiple listing board's boundaries ended at Congress Parkway (which was 500 South) even though Chicago's southern boundary *technically* extends to 138th Street. That meant no South Side properties were included in any North Side agent's searches. Furthermore, the South Side would not be included in any citywide multiple listing service until 1992.

The reality of this division meant that North Side agents did not show or sell properties south of Congress Parkway. And South Side agents did not show or sell properties north of Congress Parkway. To make matters more difficult, until the mid-90s, most brokers continued to rely on the printed listing book, which was real estate's equivalent of a Sears Christmas Catalog. Printed listing books contained the same information as today's MLS electronic database, but they were *at least* a week out of date by the time they hit the broker's office. Buyer's agents would have to call each brokerage's landline and inquire from the agent "on-floor" about that office's active listings. It was ridiculously time-consuming.

I took my licensing class at Coldwell Banker's training center in a nearby suburb of Chicago. At the time, there were no Coldwell Banker offices within the city limits. I joined Coldwell Banker after passing the State exam and was one of the first hires in their brand new office in downtown Chicago. The office was on the 87th floor of the Sears Tower (now known as Willis Tower). There was no street or "walk-in" traffic—which is kinda hard to do from the 87th floor—but we were allowed to sit "floor duty" in the building's lobby.

It was in those first few months of sitting in the lobby of the Sears Tower that I began to understand the value of a professional reputation and how it could be used to build a referral network of trusted contacts. Everyone who sat across from me at my desk was looking for an agent in the suburbs. You see, a lot of the people who worked in the Sears Tower commuted in from the suburbs to work and then went back home each evening. I began to develop a network of suburban agents that I would call and refer clients to. Once the transaction was closed, the suburban agents would mail me a referral fee. That meant that one phone call, that one trusted relationship, was suddenly worth thousands of dollars.

Referrals work both ways. As word of my solid reputation as a Coldwell Banker in-town agent began to spread, I began to receive incoming buyer and seller referrals. Many of these referrals were for North Side listings. I began going on listing appointments for properties that were in Chicago's luxury lakefront neighborhoods. And although I had the valuable "Coldwell Banker" name on my business card, it was still little ol' me standing there when the sellers opened their door—and I had to convince them I was the professional who could sell their home.

My competition in this luxury market was women my grandmother's age who sold real estate part-time—mostly to personal friends and associates. These ladies were part of a close-knit community of contemporaries that were more similar than not. I was in my early twenties, brand new to real estate, and different from this community in almost every possible way. I reasoned that the smart approach to building trust as a professional was not only to *provide* over-the-top service but to *look the part*, too. I was trying to overcome any biases and make an impression that left a lasting and positive impact.

So, I started wearing business suits and high heels to every property showing. I even bought a full-length mink coat thinking I might blend in with my colleagues a little better—it was the 80s, after all! Looking back, it makes me laugh because my fur coat payments were higher than my car payments. I had adopted the "fake it 'til you make it" style of doing business. I was looking for confidence and credibility, but what I got was a payment plan for a coat that made me look like a large rodent.

Selling real estate in the 80s was not at all like it is today. Besides using printed listing books, we also typed our contracts and then hand-delivered or snail-mailed them to all of the parties. There was no DocuSign, no email, and no fax machines yet—fax machines were gaining popularity but were not readily used in offices until the early 90s. Advertising was done through the Sunday newspaper, which only the largest brokerages could afford. There were no cell phones and no social media. The internet was still about fifteen years away.

The licensing law in Illinois required you to work for two years as a real estate agent before you could sit for the Broker's Exam. I worked for a very successful Mom and Pop brokerage in a new neighborhood just south of downtown. After several less than truthful representations, I realized that working for this brokerage could quite possibly reflect badly on my reputation, and in the worst-case scenario, possibly get me sued. In that year, I became a broker but also decided to go to law school so that I could fully understand all of the details and the ramifications of all my transactions.

Law school took three years for me to complete. I went to school in the morning and sold real estate in the afternoon and early evening. After a quick dinner, I would study until about 11:00 p.m. and then do it all again the next day. I finished my education with a JD degree and was one semester shy of my MBA. I passed the bar exam in the fall of 1991.

To some, my law degree definitely gave me more credibility. It also strengthened my reputation.

I went on to work at many national brokerage offices, including Coldwell Banker Real Estate, Century 21, ERA Properties, Rubloff Residential Real Estate (where I partnered with my sister Paula, where we were known as Holt & Holt), and Re/Max. I sold real estate on Chicago's North Side, on the Gold Coast, in Streeterville, and in Lincoln Park neighborhoods. I also sold real estate on the South Side in Hyde Park/Kenwood, South Shore, and Chicago's burgeoning downtown market. I certainly proved to myself that I could earn a living selling real estate in any Chicago neighborhood.

In 1995, I was tapped to open a new office and was assigned to recruit and train new agents. I *loved* finding new and eager agents and making sure they were fluent in the basics, clear on ethical issues, and motivated to actively seek new business.

Ten years later, I opened my own office. Training, innovative marketing, and technology made up the framework for this new venture and remain my cornerstones to this day.

But the real driving force behind my personal brand—*aka my reputation*—has always been the *three values I try to live by.*

Part Two | Values + Action = Credibility

I *love* coffee. In fact, I never start a day without it. I enjoy brewing my own mix of beans—watching the hot water pour over the bean mixture as it filters the steaming, chestnut-brown goodness into my cup always improves my mood.

In my opinion, having a well-thought-out reputation strategy is sort of like having a really good coffee filter. Just like my coffee filter, all of the business decisions I've made filter through my three core values. These three values are at the root of the trust and credibility that have created the reputation I have today.

Filtering your decisions through your core values allows you to avoid roadblocks with intention and live authentically with a clear plan and direction. Values are like the GPS for decision-making, especially tough decisions. Like GPS, values allow you to be clear on your destination and allow you to move forward while you build your reputation—and ultimately your legacy.

Operating through your values means you're completely in control, empowered by predetermined guidelines. And that no matter what happens, you have these values there to light the path and show you the way.

So, how do you compose your own set of values so that they reflect your personality and business sense? I recommend a thoughtful soul-searching session with a notebook and a pen, whereby you list ten values that you deem extraordinary.

If you find you need a little inspiration, here are some examples:

Loyalty; Spirituality; Humility; Compassion; Honesty; Kindness; Integrity; Selflessness; Determination; Generosity; Courage; Tolerance; Trustworthiness; Respect; Honor; Leadership; Equality; Authenticity; Growth; Community; Faith; Curiosity; Knowledge.

Once you've assembled a list of ten values that speak to you, narrow that list down by eliminating five of them. Once you've done that, you want to eliminate two more. Just like filtering your coffee beans through a quality filter, this type of editing will help you craft a set of values that you truly believe in.

At first, it may seem nearly impossible to pick only three values from your list, but you'll find that this editing challenge is what will make your value list so important and revered.

Make sure to search your heart for the three values that truly speak to you. You want these three values to be the three that you literally cannot imagine ever giving up or sacrificing. Another helpful trick—if you find it difficult to choose your values or edit them down to three—is to imagine the three characteristics that you value the most in others. When you interact with someone professionally, what are the personality traits that you truly admire and remember fondly?

My three values are *COMPASSION, HONESTY, and HARD WORK.*

Compassion for those that I work with, which I believe translates to kindness, respect, and professionalism at all times. Even if the other person isn't necessarily mirroring this compassion back to me, which can be a challenge.

Honesty and integrity during every transaction—no matter how large or small. I will always be truthful and transparent. I will never be deceitful or try to hide information in an effort to gain an upper hand.

And *hard work* and a healthy work ethic mean I'm always giving 100%, and I never shy away from a challenge or an intimidating task.

These are the three values I deem most important to me, and the three that I appreciate the most in others as well. I consider these three simple yet powerful values to be non-negotiable in my professional life.

For decades, these three values have never let me down. Even when another agent threw a set of keys at my pregnant belly because she was angry that an owner had decided to list with me instead of her, I remembered my values and stayed calm. Or the time I had to terminate an irate agent who had verbally intimidated a fellow female agent and then turned around and threatened me too—my core values helped me navigate that stressful situation professionally without tarnishing my reputation. Even through these challenging times, having my values firmly front-and-center meant that I continued on my successful track, while these other agents are no longer practicing.

So let's take a moment to talk about your professional reputation. In any line of work, reputation is important. Of course it is. But I would argue that it's perhaps nowhere more important than in the real estate world. When selling or renting real estate, you have your product, which is the property, and you have yourself. And that's about it.

Your personal brand and reputation are absolutely paramount to your ultimate success.

Reputation is a finely tuned strategy that's built on your core values and how you want to be remembered. What lies between your values and your reputation is the path, actions, relationships, and judgments that form the world's perception of you.

Just like that coffee filter I mentioned earlier, your "value filter" is what flavors everything you do, how you behave, and ultimately how you are perceived and remembered by colleagues, customers, and clients.

Then, through your reputation, you are leveraging your influence and directing your audience towards the narrative you want them to have. It's not about the smoke and mirrors or the "fake-it-till-you-make-it" fur coat strategy I employed at the beginning of my career. Although I can look back and laugh about it now, employing an empty strategy like that will only serve to distract your audience.

Your professional reputation is rooted in trust and credibility, which springs from your values and your passions.

The good news is that you are ultimately in control. No matter what comes your way, your three values will keep you on track.

Part Three | A Very Happy Host

As a successful Chicago real estate professional for nearly four decades, my experience has branched out to include so many different areas. Although I started in the traditional buyer/seller experience, I've since worked with savvy investors, beloved non-profit organizations, affordable housing complexes, luxurious homes in premier neighborhoods, brand new construction, and repurposed condominium conversions. And I've also branched out into the burgeoning short-term rental space, which has proved to be a particularly rewarding and lucrative experience.

These days, that brand new agent in the fur coat sitting in the lobby of the Sears Tower back in 1985 would be happy to see that she's still working for herself and is in total control of how much she earns. (She would also be overjoyed to see that in 2021, the Chicago Association of Realtors elected its first Black female president, and they elected their second in 2022!)

And she would be so excited to see the growth of the short-term rental market and see just how far that particular branch has blossomed.

Short-term rental hosting was successful pre-pandemic but is one of those particularly lucky areas that has exploded and actually grown during the pandemic. Most people have found that they prefer to have a bit more space than the typical hotel can provide, and they have turned to Airbnb and VRBO to rent houses and condominiums instead. In fact, I've had such personal success with and have so enjoyed my short-term rental hosting career, I have started a coaching and training program to guide others to becoming successful hosts themselves.

Becoming a short-term rental host opened up a whole new world for my real estate career, and I love sharing this knowledge with others. I've also enjoyed how all of the skills I've developed over my decades as a successful agent—namely staging, copywriting, photography, marketing, and customer service—are the skills that make me a successful host and host instructor, too.

In fact, one of my favorite parts of my career today involves teaching and coaching agents, investors, and the "host-curious" all about maximizing the short-term rental potential of their properties.

I also love how the three core values I live by in my real estate career —*compassion, honesty, and hard work*—also effortlessly apply to being a short-term rental host as well.

I'm living proof that a compassionate, honest, and hard-working host will be a successful host.

If you're at all "host-curious" then I encourage you to reach out and get in touch! Just this past year, I founded *The Happy Host Academy*, an online short-term rental resource space that is filled to the brim with information and coaching opportunities to help you.

There are *1:1 coaching opportunities* where you and I will work together to create a personalized plan that reflects your goals and lifestyle. Then there are the *group coaching classes* where you'll create your five-star property listing in a supportive, team-like atmosphere. And I also offer *online courses* that allow you to pursue the possibility of hosting on your own schedule and at your own pace.

So no matter where you're at with your hosting journey, whether you're just getting started, want to take your hosting to the next level, or aren't even quite sure yet that hosting is for you, The Happy Host Academy has your back.

Pam Holt, Coldwell Banker 1985.

Pam Holt and Paula Holt, Rubloff Residential Real Estate.

ABOUT PAM HOLT

Pam Holt (aka The Happy Host) has worked for nearly four decades as a real estate broker/attorney and has landed in some of the most successful brokerages in Chicago. Just when she thought her professional life couldn't be any more fulfilling, she dipped her toe into the short-term rental waters, and a whole new world opened up. As a host, Pam discovered an entirely new facet of successful real estate investment. Being a host also allowed her to share her love for her city in a more profound and satisfying way. She discovered she has a knack for short-term rental hosting, and it quickly became another passion. If you check out her Instagram account (*@thehappyhostacademy*), you'll see that she is an avid design enthusiast and a fierce supporter of women-owned businesses. Look a little closer and you'll find that she travels the world with her daughters, while guests pay the tab. To say she's got a lot on her plate is a bit of an understatement, but Pam wouldn't have it any other way. Her belief in what she does keeps her energized and excited about the future. She continues to assist real estate clients looking to purchase short-term rental properties, runs a successful short-term rental business of her own, and teaches others how to have their own liberating and lucrative hosting careers. Pam is a proud mom of two wonderful girls and an active crusader in the fight to end breast cancer. You can see her and her daughter on a poster for the national Avon Walk campaign, an accomplishment of which she's particularly proud. Drop Pam a line and say hello and let her know if she can help with any short-term rental questions you have.

Linktree: *www.linktr.ee/thehappyhostacademy*

6   PLAXY BUDZINSKA

 "Our destiny is not written for us, but by us."

BARACK OBAMA FOR PRESIDENT IN 2012

I was unsure what I would write; it has taken me a little while to figure this out. My initial intention was to write solely about my business reputation, but I quickly realised that there was more to being important.

In the early noughties, my family and I lived abroad, and we were fortunate to meet incredible people and form lifelong friendships. We had so much fun working and living aboard that we thought we would never return home. But after a while, I started to miss England. So finally, after almost fourteen years of living in three unique countries, we were ready to come home. Although I must admit, I was only prepared to go home because of some very sage women with whom I had surrounded myself for seven years at our last posting in Beijing.

One particular woman comes to mind, Shayn Hermen, my neighbour. Our front doors faced each other, and when our doors were open, we could see each other's back gardens. That made us laugh a lot. When we moved into our home, and the initial moving-in chaos had settled, Shayn introduced me to an extraordinary coffee morning community.

Coffee mornings were opportunities for us in the community to check up on each other, make sure no one was having a tough time, and right the world. On one coffee morning, several ladies announced they were leaving and returning to their countries of origin, most because they were empty nesters and it was time for spouses to retire. I had never heard the term "empty nester" before, so I had to ask what an "empty nester" was. "Plaxy, it's when the kids leave home for university or not, or you kick them out of your house permanently, and they never come back home." Ahh, that made sense. I was then asked if I was prepared for an empty nest. Nope, that was my answer. So this is where the learning began.

New Learnings: "If you are afraid to fail, you are afraid to succeed."

I started learning about buying property in the UK in the mornings over coffee. I also learnt about hurdles we would have to overcome to purchase a property. Obtaining a mortgage, for example, would be easier with a credit rating. We had spent a lot of time away from our home country and had no history of spending time in the UK. This made it difficult for lenders to assess if we were creditworthy. This knowledge was beneficial because it helped me prepare for our return to our home country. To create a credit rating, we returned home regularly to have a purchasing history. The second issue for me was that I preferred to live in a house, whereas my husband preferred to live in an apartment; I lost the argument, and we decided to buy an apartment instead.

Most of the ladies at the coffee mornings had side hustles. These ladies grew into thriving international businesswomen. We had ladies who loved furniture hunting for personal use and turned their passion into international antique furniture specialists. Others loved buying and collecting semi-precious stones and pearls for unique jewellery. They also grew their craft into some of the region's best bespoke jewellery companies. One lady loved reading books but did not know what to do with them once she finished reading. So, she started a second-hand English bookshop, and all proceeds from book sales were donated to some of the local orphanages to replace worn-out furniture. She then realised how difficult it was to find furniture supplies and decided that instead of orphanages looking for furniture, she would find, store, and deliver. She grew to be the largest furniture supplier for orphanages in Beijing. I saw how much care the ladies put into providing a product or service. However, what impressed me the most was how driven they were and how they became trusted there. They taught me the importance of you as a brand and how important your reputation is for your brand.

Putting yourself first

Moving forward, in 2015, by chance, in conversation with friends, I heard about a company that taught you about different property income streams. I was curious, so I researched this property school in Peterborough, England, and it blew my mind. I registered for the three-day masterclass, and that was the best £3000.00 I had ever spent in my whole life. In those three days, I came away with three property business models I wanted to pursue: HMOs (houses of multiple occupancies), short-term rentals (serviced accommodations), and residential development.

The HMO Project

I'll start with the HMO project. I had to learn about this particular business model because I had never heard of it before, so I jumped onto a year-long programme. Most of my family and friends thought I was being duped and would get burnt. I understood why they felt that way; the property business is not for thin-skinned people, and the HMO model is synonymous with student accommodation. As you may know, student accommodation reputation is not ranked at the top to own as an investor; the running costs can be very steep and your ROI can be compromised. It can be brutal; there are many casualties to attest to this. I wanted to do the HMO model for young professionals, to bridge that gap between leaving university and your parents not wanting you to go back home. In my head, I am providing a service to parents whose kids are still struggling with managing their finances and are not ready to take on the costs and pressure of managing an apartment. I had found my ideal tenants and knew who would pay the rent. The parents would finance my young professionals' rent, possibly for the first two years, before they move on or the parents cut the bursary department. All I needed to do next was find the finance to purchase a house to convert into an HMO.

At this point, our original property purchase, the three-bedroom apartment, had gained enough equity, so I refinanced and purchased a house for my HMO. Before I could buy the house, I had to do my due diligence on the location, style, price, and ideal tenant. Although I first looked for a suitable property to renovate in my immediate local area, I needed help finding the right house style. I was mindful that the government was introducing new electrical and room size laws.

Hence, the property had to be something I could strip down to the carcass, rewire, and move bathrooms and toilets around. I had never stripped a house before, and my mistakes are still traumatising today. Nevertheless, I finished the job and am very proud of my first renovation. I spent quite a fair amount of money on my doer upper. This is what I believe. Every property I have or manage must have the approval of your caring grandmother. Why? Because as a landlord, I want to ensure you have space, security, independence, and privacy. That is Ravens House Assets Ltd.'s ethos and mission. (*www.rhsa.uk*).

The renovations for the HMO were completed in August, which is the wrong time to find tenants because everyone is on holiday here in the UK and Europe. I had just pumped so much money in, and the house was vacant with no viewings. Oh, hell, I started to panic, and all eyes from family and friends were on me, ready with the "I told you so" expression, and I needed to do something swiftly. I had a ta-da moment, a short-term rental. My HMO is near a teaching hospital, so I created a new Facebook account and posted a small advertisement targeting the local area. At this point, I had no idea what I was doing in serviced accommodations; I had no training at all. Oops, I still need to explain how an HMO works. For each bedroom in the house, you supply beds and wardrobes, bedside tables and lamps, and sometimes small bedroom fridges (not everyone does that, but I do). I even had duvets, pillows, towels, etc., for my new tenants. Thinking about it now, my HMO was set up for serviced accommodation. Oh, that's funny. Anyway, the Facebook ad went out, and within twenty-four hours, I got two bookings. I was so shocked at how much money I had made that month. It covered my August and September costs and two-thirds of the expenses. With that said, I could have implemented the serviced accommodation business model with the house long-term. Instead, I decided to stick with my original plan of renting the rooms to young professionals. However, there was a greater need in the community for that service. The HMO was fully booked by the end of October 2016 and has remained so ever since.

The Beast with Two Heads: Serviced Accommodation

Where to start…I had heard about the rent-to-rent (subleasing, as some will call it) business model, where you lease a property from a landlord and find clients/tenants to occupy the unit. I am not going into the legalities or moral debate of the rights or wrongs of having short-term rental properties in a community. All I know is that I provide a vital service to a migrant community. In my first book, *Hospitable Hosts*, I wrote about the two hats you must wear once you get into serviced accommodation. You start with property management, which requires financing to purchase or lease a property. This is investment-heavy initially, and then you transition to labour-intensive hospitality. However, I found the property side of the business less stressful because buying or leasing a property is already a well-structured process. The checklist is easy to follow for financing, legal, and contractors. The majority of people you meet are "one-time relationships."

On the other hand, the hospitality side of serviced accommodation is still in its infancy as an industry, and navigating the different processes is overwhelming, especially if you are new to the business. But this is the fun side of the company on two fronts. First, a person-to-person environment helps you build relationships by engaging with clients. Second,

I get a kick out of showing off what my community has to offer. For example, great restaurants, spas and gyms, sports clubs, schools, evening life, and places where guests can unwind.

We have built a reputation as the "go-to" for short stays in our local area. However, I have to explain something before I tell you why we are the go-to for short visits in our area. We are UK-based, and most real estate and letting agents only provide long-stay services as part of their business model. Hence, the short-stay market is a niche market still growing in the UK. However, though laws are being introduced to slow down the industry's fast growth, there is a caveat.

How to be the "go-to" business in serviced accommodations in your community

Introducing myself to the local real estate agents was a good start because they always have clients looking for properties to buy or rent. So I invited as many local real estate agents to see the property I had just completed refurbishing and explained my business model. Every agent who took the time to visit the property was impressed by the quality and high standard. And the second thing they asked me was that when the time came for the landlord to sell, I could call them first to get the landlord on their books. Most of the leased properties were referred to me privately. I also invited professional photographers to use the place as a staging studio. Finally, I asked private chefs to visit the apartment and advise on the kitchenware they would use if asked to come and prepare an intimate meal for guests. With this done, a buzz was created within the community about my services. Not only that, I had a ready-made list of services for my guests.

We are now in the year 2023

This has been a wild journey. We are now a seven-figure business and growing. I knew I could do it; however, self-doubt was always on my heels. I have always wanted to expand my serviced accommodation business to the continent of Africa, particularly in sub-Saharan Africa. Guess what? Zambia, Lusaka, is our ground zero. I come from Zambia, so it only makes sense to start there. Africa has so many languages. One of the essential principles in finding a property for STR is "location, location, location." I have a new one for you: language, language, language, if you are crossing continents. Conducting market research to get insights into the tastes and habits of local clients is necessary before expanding a short-term property rental business into a new market such as Africa. I did both; this study can be conducted online or in physical locations.

I found significant advantages to conducting research online, including time and money savings. Research done online can be done anywhere in the world and involves fewer resources than research done on the ground; it is an alternative that is more cost-effective for restricted budgets. In addition, conducting research online made it possible to access large amounts of data in a short amount of time. I was able to evaluate and spot patterns and opportunities in the target market. I uncovered client behaviour patterns and buying preferences through data analysis and research tools and locked down my niche market.

However, it's not all bells and whistles; internet research has certain restrictions. For example, it is frequently restricted to readily available data, which may need to be more accurate or sufficient. In addition, a study conducted online might give a partial picture of the local environment and the cultural subtleties of the target market, which could lead to unsuitable or wrong judgments. In addition, there is frequently the possibility of "information overload," which occurs when there is an excessive amount of useless data, making it difficult to draw meaningful conclusions.

On the other hand, research on the ground enabled me to obtain first-hand knowledge of the market and a deeper understanding of the cultural subtleties of the community. I got a more in-depth grasp of the local business environment, traditions, and regulations by travelling to the local market and speaking with suppliers, rivals, and potential consumers. This helped me modify my services better to suit the requirements and preferences of the local and global markets.

However, research on location was both time-consuming and costly. When entering a new market, businesses must set aside money to cover the costs of travel, lodging, and other associated charges. Nonetheless, my on-the-ground research revealed how scalable this business model was for expansion into multiple areas.

There was a good mix between the benefits and drawbacks of doing research online and in the real world. The on-the-ground study gave me a more comprehensive and nuanced view of the local market, whereas internet research is more convenient and cost-effective. Companies or businesses in the short-term rental industry looking to enter new areas like Africa should employ a hybrid of the two approaches.

A crucial element in the success of a short-term rental business is building a solid reputation in the market. Building a reputation and trust in the community helps businesses attract more customers and ensure repeat business. Utilizing your life experiences and expertise in your short-term rental business is one strategy to do this. By providing lessons, workshops, or equipment rentals, you may combine your enthusiasm for a specific interest or activity into your rental experience. By doing this, you not only provide your visitors with a special and customised experience, but you also build a solid brand identity that appeals to the area.

Making a referral programme for nearby business partners is a highly successful technique for further growing your brand and increasing awareness. For instance, the coaching, mentoring, and training programme offered by Ravens House Assets for launching and expanding your short-term rental business can include a referral programme that rewards community business partners for referring their visitors to the programme. Ravens House Assets can make use of the network of surrounding businesses to extend its reach and draw in additional prospects by offering incentives like discounts or rewards for recommendations.

A referral programme also fosters a sense of community and strong partnerships with other businesses. By partnering with other neighbourhood companies, you position yourself as a valued resource and partner for business owners wishing to launch and expand their short-term rental operation. The referral programme may foster a spirit of cooperation and support among local business owners as well as help establish confidence and credibility with potential customers.

In conclusion, building a solid reputation in the neighbourhood is crucial for a short-term rental business to succeed. Using your talents and life experiences may help you create a special and personalised visitor experience, and a referral programme for neighbourhood business partners can help you grow your company and build solid ties with the locals. Businesses may establish a successful short-term rental business that is designed to last by concentrating on developing a strong brand identity and utilising the strength of local connections.

Don't hesitate to get in touch with me at *www.linktr.ee/PlaxyBudzinska* if you want to know more about me and how I can help people start and grow a successful short-term and mid-term rental portfolio, or if you are a real estate investor or management and maintenance company and want to connect with me.

ABOUT PLAXY BUDZINSKA

Ravens House Assets Limited is a UK-based property investment and management firm run by Plaxy Budzinska, focusing on HMOs (houses in multiple occupancies) and STR (short-term rental) properties. Plaxy has been helping investors and property managers for more than ten years, so she knows exactly what problems they face.

Living and working in various foreign locations helped her become a serial entrepreneur. As someone who has always been comfortable in social situations, she quickly found work in Beijing. She did event planning and communication for an international school group and the Embassy of the Republic of Zambia in China. And now that she's a committed property public speaker, published author, coach, and mentor, specialising in HMOs and STRs, she's on a mission to maximize your earnings through direct reservations. She is an entrepreneur with a wide range of skills and interests and wants to connect with others who share her enthusiasm for global issues. She is a seasoned property trainer with a strong work ethic. She helps property managers and investors in short-term rentals get their businesses off the ground and flourish.

Rather than focusing on material possessions, she emphasises making the most of the resources at your disposal.

Website: *www.ravenshouse.co.uk*
Linktr.ee: *www.linktr.ee/PlaxyBudzinska*

7 STACEY PARETTI RASE

Whenever you think of professions or industries that traditionally have been known throughout the years as being driven by reputation, I'm sure car dealers aren't the first thing to come to mind. I wouldn't even be surprised if you chuckled when you read that intro. Yet, that's the business my family has been in now for five generations. I grew up in New Orleans, Louisiana, in a family of automobile dealers. My great-grandfather started the company in the 1930s, with humble beginnings by opening his own service shop. Later he made the leap to a sales franchise and my grandfather, father, brother, and husband followed suit. Nearly ninety years later after my great-grandfather began, my own son is working in the business, soon to be followed by his cousins.

Why am I bringing up the car business in a book focused on reputation in the real estate and rental industry? Because our family didn't survive this long in a climate and culture that tends to joke about and even mistrust car dealers. On the contrary. We have built our name and brand first and foremost around our reputation. Remaining loyal to our current customers has always been at the forefront of our family business model. And what we've called the "Paretti Pledge" for decades has been our guiding light. The pillars of the pledge are to provide a customized experience for every customer that considers their lifestyle, budget, and preferences.

While I did not decide to build a career in the family car business, I took away countless lessons from it. My greatest job in life has been (and still is!) that of mom. While raising them, I also enjoyed a career in journalism, as a newspaper reporter, columnist, freelance writer, magazine editor, and high school journalism teacher. When our fourth child was a high school senior and I was approaching being an empty nester, I decided to take a shot at running short-term rentals. And I've never looked back!

I'm not one to call my properties "Airbnbs." I have my homes listed across multiple platforms and have proudly grown my business to where 60% of my guests book directly with me and not through OTAs (online travel agencies such as Airbnb, VRBO, etc.) But let's face it. When it comes to short-term rentals, most of us began by listing our spaces first on Airbnb. And for most hosts, Airbnb continues to be our most reliable source for bookings. But what started out as a platform focused on community, a shared economy model, and good will has become a behemoth of a business. Which is great! I own stock lol. But with the corporate enterprise came the millions who signed on to list their homes and spaces without much regard to their neighbors. They got in it for the quick buck and are not running their businesses with a true host mentality at heart.

I plugged in a few keywords into Google years ago so that I could be alerted when anything new popped up on the topics of Airbnb, VRBO, and Short-Term Rentals (to name a few). What resulted was a barrage of email alerts to my inbox each day touting mostly the bad news surrounding our industry. The internet is rife with stories on increased STR regulations, horror stories about parties and damage, the negative impact STRs may have on local housing markets, and even court cases involving bad hosts and bad guests alike. It goes on and on.

And that's why I decided to contribute to this book. My goal is to upend the bad reputation of short-term rentals. Not just in my community, but worldwide. There are so many things that we can be doing as hosts to dispel myths and change opinions! I believe that the majority of us (this means you, if you've cared enough to pick up this book and read it) are in this industry to do GOOD. And if enough of us band together to spread the word, I know we can make a difference in the reputation of the STR industry, one host at a time.

I've been hosting for four years now, and I own and operate five listings in my city. I've worked very hard to build my reputation as a responsible host who supports and respects my community. The most grass roots way to do this is by staying active in networking or business groups in your city. Join your region's Chamber of Commerce and go to the meetups! You'll be amazed at how many connections and relationships you can build just by going old school and handing out your business card and sharing your story. If your city has a dedicated Business Associ-ation, join that as well. You'll get to introduce yourselves to other busi-ness owners who live and work around your properties, as well as stay on top of topics in your city that may affect you, such as legislation and regulations.

Partnering with local businesses is also a simple yet effective way to have your business' good reputation spread throughout the community. I purchase small gift cards to local coffee shops and restaurants near my rentals and leave them for guests as a "surprise and delight" upon check in. I also have a section in my guest books that includes local restaurant menus. (Of course, we also have a digital guidebook that includes personal recommendations and links, but some guests prefer to view menus the old-fashioned way.) There's another section in the guest book that includes discount cards/codes for local businesses. Our guests always comment on these small, thoughtful touches. You may be think-ing, "Ok, but what's in it for me?" The answer is that the connections you make with local business owners is golden. They appreciate that you are sending clients their way and they won't hesitate to speak highly of you and your rentals.

Take it a few steps further. Like and follow all of the businesses around your properties on social media. Dedicate some time each week to not only look at their posts and "like" them, but comment on them every now and then and share them on your own account stories when you think the post may be intriguing to your guests. You'll find that if you do this consistently, the businesses will not only follow you back, but they will also start to share your posts at times. Hey...you've just created some community juju! One local business near me posts an end of the year wrap up on Instagram of the top 10 most influential/supportive fellow businesses and they selected my properties for 2022. Something must be working!

If you're so inclined and have the time, pick a local business to highlight each week on your own social media. I like to do "Tuesday Tastings" where I visit a local restaurant each Tuesday and post some photos or reels highlighting the business. Or focus on some non-profits in your town that can use some additional exposure. This might seem taboo... but I suggest even highlighting and supporting other local short-term rentals in your town. I've become great friends with other hosts in my area and we frequently send referrals to each other when we are booked but guests need spaces to stay. One of the most incredible things I've learned about people in this industry is how willing they are to help one another. When one wins, we all win!

And while you're collaborating with other local hosts, don't forget to share your recommendations for incredible vendors in our industry who help our businesses thrive. Do you have a reliable and trustworthy housekeeper, handyman, plumber, electrician, HVAC or appliance tech that you consider your "go-to"? Then shout it from the rooftops! Let your fellow hosts and property managers know about them. Tell your family and friends. These professionals are invaluable, so give them the credit they deserve and help them grow their own businesses with other clients who will equally respect them. I know I could NOT run my business seamlessly without these men and women. I heard a story from a fellow host in Michigan who was battling with proposed STR regulations in her area that would severely affect her bottom line. When her plumber heard about it, he attended a city council meeting and spoke on behalf of the STRs and the hosts in the city who employed him. He gave testament to the economic impact the STR industry had on his bottom line. The proposed increased regulation movement did not ultimately pass. Sometimes it's the small things we do tending our good reputation with other businesses that can make a big difference in the long run.

One of the reasons I absolutely adore hosting is that I get to share my incredible city with others. I've lived in St. Tammany Parish (we call our counties parishes here in Louisiana) since I was five years old. St. Tammany is called "New Orleans' Northshore" as we are separated from the city by a singular twenty-four-mile-long bridge across Lake Pontchartrain (the longest continuous bridge over water in the world. It's in Guinness. Go GTS*). I grew up here and have been a part of the community for nearly five decades. The New Orleans region is known for its fun-loving atmosphere—Laissez le bons rouler y'all!—and I've spent my life enjoying big annual events like Mardi Gras, Jazz Fest, the Sugar Bowl, and French Quarter Fest, to name a few. But it's the smaller, more home-grown events and festivals that I love sharing most with my guests. Our city of Covington hosts special events like live concerts monthly by the riverside where locals and tourists alike bring picnic blankets and bottles of wine to enjoy the atmosphere. Or our annual Three Rivers Art Festival, which spans multiple city blocks and showcases juried artists from all over the country. Every week there's some sort of cultural arts event in our area and I wanted my guests to be privy to what's going on just a block or two away while they are visiting. So, I spoke with the Director of Special Events in our city and proposed that there be a QR code created that leads people to the city's calendar of updated events. The code is now proudly displayed for all our guests to see so they can enjoy the unique events in our great city (and it's available to other areas businesses to display in their spaces!)

Another way to connect with your community is to participate in auctions with local non-profits. But don't just give away a night or weekend stay! Instead, partner with local businesses to create a bundle prize that includes a night's stay or discount at your property with a shopping spree...a delicious dinner...a brunch...a kayak tour...a yoga class...an in-home massage...a wine tasting...The possibilities are endless! Create a display board to set on a table easel at the auction, along with a

QR code or business cards so that attendees at the event can get more information on your business even if they don't bid on the item.

I understand that most of the information I've shared at this point is grounded in marketing. That's because I truly believe that if you are running your STR business with a reputable foundation then your marketing will speak for itself. Others in your community will want to partner with you. They will want to recommend you. They will want to promote you. It's not rocket science. It's just being a conscientious host who truly cares about being a part of your neighborhood and then knowing that your neighbors have your back. Period.

After I had a few years of hosting under my belt, I applied to become an Airbnb Superhost Ambassador. It's become one of the most fulfilling aspects of my hosting journey. I get connected with new hosts who are just in the beginning stages of developing their listing and I'm able to coach them up until they welcome their first guests through their doors. I've coached hundreds of new hosts; some as close as in my hometown and others as far away as the Middle East and Africa. I find it personally rewarding to help new hosts navigate in the very beginning. I remember how anxious I was before welcoming my first guests. I remember how clueless I was about licensing...taxes...operations...messaging...folding a fitted sheet...all of it! I understand that these new hosts are feeling most of those same things and I'm able to walk them through things one step at a time. On a broader level, I also believe that my interactions with them is helping to build up the reputation of short-term rentals and their operators. I coach these hosts from the very beginning to treat their venture as the business that it is, to always consider things through their guests' lens, and to always be aware of how their actions (or inactions) affect their reputation in the communities where they operate.

My newest venture is volunteering as a Community Host Leader for Airbnb. I lead and moderate a Facebook group for hosts across south Louisiana. Our goal is to bring hosts together to build a thriving community of hospitality entrepreneurs who collaborate, share, and collectively grow. We advocate for short term rentals in our communities and share best practices on how to add positively to the conversation.

At the time of this writing our group is in its beginning stages. But something I'm really excited to introduce to our group is a project that I began in my business a couple of years ago. I took a tour of our local Food Bank and the director educated me on the immense need for food in our community. I immediately thought of all the non-perishable food that my guests often leave behind after checking out. I left that tour with a few hundred brown paper bags that had the Food Bank's logo on the front. Then I crafted up a letter that I stapled to each bag. It welcomes them to our home and to our city. It urges them to shop for the two-for-one deals on their grocery run and to place the extra items in the bag and leave it on the counter at check out. I thank them for helping to support the need in our area and for contributing to our community during their stay.

I have been overwhelmed by my guests' response to this simple call to action. And it's so simple! I can only imagine the incredible impact we could make as hosts if each of us started the initiative in communities around the world. I encourage any host reading this to contact your local Food Bank and get this started in your own property. And let me know the response you receive!

Giving back to community and to those who are underserved or less fortunate was engrained in me from an early age. My mom spent all her adult life in various aspects of volunteerism and philanthropy. She was a unique force and change maker who taught my brother and me that your reputation ultimately isn't who you are, it's who you serve. I could write a whole other chapter just on the good deeds she did throughout her life, both large and small. Some of them were public and recognized. She served as volunteer Chair of the Board at our city's local hospital for three decades. She spearheaded the formation of a Children's Advocacy Center in our region where abused children have a place to tell their stories and receive examination by caring professionals in a safe, warm environment instead of a sterile hospital room or police station. She worked tirelessly for years to get a home built in our community to serve as a day center for homeless families to seek shelter, use facilities, and receive professional counseling to help them secure permanent housing. These are just three examples of the "big" things she did. But when she died a few years ago and I stood at the front of the church receiving well-wishers before her funeral, I was struck by the countless people who came to tell stories of how my mother changed their lives. The majority were people I had never met, nor had she ever spoken about them. But she had affected their lives in deep and meaningful ways, and they wanted to come show their love and respect for her. It was dizzying listening to their stories. She had always told me that her biggest joy wasn't giving someone a handout, it was giving them a hand UP. Hundreds of people were testament that day that she had done exactly that.

Years later, that day center I mentioned is named in her honor. And I received a call recently that a new fire station is being built in our city and it will be named after her. I know she would be extremely honored. But I also know she never did any of those things for the recognition. It's ironic to know that her volunteer efforts in our community were never done with her outward reputation in mind, but that her legacy now carries with it a reputation of committed service and love for helping others.

I've tried to carry my mom's torch in my own small ways. I've found myself in a unique position with my rentals to be able to offer up spaces for families who are in need. I've opened my doors to victims of domestic violence at no charge. I now volunteer with that same non-profit (Family Promise) that built the day center for homeless families and offer up my homes to families in need who are in emergent situations of transition. And I'm in the early stages of talks with a non-profit called Heart Gift to see how I may be able to assist their cause. Their mission is to provide life-saving heart surgery to children around the world. Their local chapter is robust and has amazing surgeons who donate their time and talents to ill children. But these families need places to stay when they visit for the surgery and recovery. If I can block out even one week a year to offer my homes, then that's something.

I know not everyone in our industry may be able to make such concessions on their calendar, but I encourage every host and business owner to look for ways, whether big or small, to affect positive change in your community and around the real estate profession in general. Our reputations depend on it.

*To learn more about Family Promise, visit *www.familypromise.org*. To learn more about Heart Gift, visit *www.heartgift.org*. Still wondering what GTS is? Just Google That "Stuff."

ABOUT STACEY PARETTI RASE

Stacey Paretti Rase is the CEO and founder of Rare Find Rentals, offering short term rentals just outside of New Orleans, Louisiana. After a successful career in freelance writing and editing, Stacey began hosting when her four children flew the coop and left her an empty nester. She lovingly refers to her first short term rental, Lacroix Loft + Landings, as her fifth child. Stacey now operates five listings on the north shore of New Orleans and has over 1,000 five-star reviews. Her newest venture is Sleepy Lagoon, an eighteen-acre property with river access that features ponds and lagoons winding around the three separate homes on site. It's the perfect setting for bridal parties, family reunions, girlfriend getaways, and special small events. Hosting bridal party stays has become Stacey's specialty. She offers unique amenities and stages her spaces to ensure her brides and grooms have everything they need for the big day. She has also learned how best to market her spaces to entice bridal bookings and coaches other hosts on how to best emerge into the bridal hosting market. Stacey was a contributing author in the Amazon best-selling book *Hospitable Hosts* and has been featured on numerous podcasts, including Thanks For Visiting, The STR Sisterhood, and Boostly's Behind The Host. Stacey serves as an Airbnb Superhost Ambassador and an Airbnb Community Host Leader. She and her husband Mike live in Covington, Louisiana, with their two pups Tipsy and Eddy. When she's not scrubbing toilets, messaging guests, or folding incessant piles of laundry, she can be found reading, peeling crawfish, or trying not to lose on the tennis court.

Links: *www.linktr.ee/rarefindrentals*

8 CHRIS LEDWIDGE

When I graduated high school, the first thing I wanted to do was move out of my parents' house. And I knew I had to get a job. Whatever job that was, it had to pay me enough money to live on my own and pay my bills. And the only jobs that were hiring young high schoolers were jobs serving tables.

After working in the restaurant industry into my mid-twenties, I quickly realized this was not my career path. Two of my close friends, Nate Borghi and Cory Tona, were getting into mortgages. I watched them go through the process of getting into the industry. And they always came back to me when playing golf together, saying, *"You have to do this! You are going to be so good at it, you just don't know yet. This whole business is you. This is designed for the way your brain works and how you solve problems. You're going to love it."*

I studied for my national state exams for MLS originations and passed.

However, when I got out of high school, I didn't know what I wanted to do. I didn't necessarily want to go work in the hospital. My mom was an RN with the VA hospital for thirty-five years. She was constantly pushing me in that direction, and it didn't feel right.

So, here I am going through nursing school at Riverside Community College, the LVN-RN Bridge program, and BAM, I find out I'm having a daughter! Now I have got to commit to something, and it's got to be 100%.

I'm either going to commit to completing this LVN-RN Bridge program and becoming an RN or I am going to pivot now and commit to mortgage banking, and originating loans and see where I can go with that. It was at this moment I decided to go down the loan origination path.

Nursing just wasn't my calling.

By this time, my two friends were in the mortgage industry, and they knew my personality and knew I'd love originating loans. I like the mortgage business because there are no boundaries. It's not a salary job so there's no ceiling. I was going to be rewarded for my efforts and commitment, and that's what I wanted.

The mortgage industry gave me that opportunity to use my natural born skillset, whether it's communication, explaining complex situations in a very easy-to-digest way, customer service, or genuinely helping people. The industry was like serving tables. It was all about giving a good experience and helping people get what they want.

Early on in my career, most of my originations were done with home builders, like Lennar Homes, KB Homes, and TriPointe Homes. I worked with them in the capacity of a backup lender. Meaning, each one of those builders has their in-house mortgage lender. Anytime you go to buy a house from those builders, they push you to their in-house lender and say, *"Hey, you have to get pre-qualified with Lender XYZ. If you use them, we're gonna pay you a seller credit of $5,000. Okay?"*

Now, those in-house lenders would oftentimes run into problems with the loans they're looking to originate for buyers. And they would have to decline or turn them down.

When in-house lenders would decline the loans, that's where I came in. Most of my growth in this business came from originating loans for home builders in a backup capacity.

So, I would get people who were just declined a loan and received terrible news they're not going to be able to purchase a home for their children. These people are super stressed at this point and on an emotional rollercoaster.

The builder would say, *"Call Chris!"*

I had a gift for handling their emotions, helping them focus and communicate with me so we could find a solution and get them financing to buy the home they wanted.

And over time, that became my reputation!

My reputation became that I was going to get the deal closed and done on time. This is when I learned the value of building a good reputation. When I started with one builder and built a good reputation, that started to spread to other home builders and allowed me to rapidly scale my business and production.

It was the reputation of getting it done, great service, closing on time, putting these people in a compromised emotional state, getting them to calm down and focus, communicate with me, so I can get them into the home!

And the gratification of those people... I was honored to serve them.

I worked with countless U.S. veterans on VA loans that were turned down, countless FHA loans that were turned down, numerous down payment assistance loans that were turned down, as well as countless difficult conventional financing loans.

The idea of a home being yanked away from you and your family, you've not yet told them the bad news, and all your energy is relying on one person to solve the problem. I became good at carrying that weight and building that reputation.

I enjoyed it too!

The people knew we were working hard to get them into a home. Once they moved into their home, we would receive pictures, gift baskets... and it was pure gratitude. I was having a really good time at that point in my career, learning and understanding what reputation meant to me personally as an originator for the company. And that's where I started learning the value of being reputation driven.

A mortgage lender is like an entrepreneur, and I'm equally passionate about being an entrepreneur and serving others. What always drew me to become an entrepreneur was the idea of being able to build something, exercise strategies, create, make mistakes, and grow. And in a nursing environment, I just felt like I would only be of service and hold value by contributing back to society in a positive way.

All great...

But the fire inside me to be an entrepreneur and exercise strategies, ideas, and build something great wasn't going to be there as a nurse.

In my first two years in the mortgage business, I quickly realized that what I learned while taking the classes and MLS testing has very little bearing on my day-to-day job as a loan originator. In those first two years, I knew nothing and no one!

My two friends that worked at other mortgage companies were doing their thing, but I couldn't call them every day and get my problem solved. So those first two years I had to figure it out on my own.

What's an APR and how do I explain that?

What's an amortization schedule? What's the difference?

What's an ARM in the index?

All these things I had no clue about. I feared having conversations with people in those first two years because I didn't want to come across as if I didn't know what I was talking about.

As a new loan originator, you must commit to trying to understand the ins and outs of these loan programs and learn how to produce the best loans possible.

When getting started in the mortgage business, you should try to build a database of contacts and clients so that if you ever need them, you will know where to find them. You should have a stack of business cards and a binder of loan program guidelines. You will need to be well prepared because your goal is to get any realtor to refer you to a loan or take fifteen minutes out of their day to talk with you over lunch or a phone call.

And when you get those first couple meetings with realtors, you're going to fumble, you're going to say the wrong things, but you need to move past any mistakes you feel that you're making and try to close more deals and do some reps.

So, for those first two years, it was just me showing and proving my abilities to close loans, getting one referral partner at a time, getting one loan done at a time, and testing every strategy and idea I had, learning what worked, and what didn't.

During these first two years, my daughter reached about nine months old. I had $75 left on my credit card and $1,500 in my checking account. I had to go to my brother and borrow $2,000 to make sure that all the bills were paid that month.

And, you know what?

I didn't panic because I could see the work I had put in over those two years starting to pay off. I saw a pipeline building of business and it was coming in, and I knew that all I had to do was hang tight and get to the next round and everything would be okay. It certainly got stressful. But I never lost my head because I could see that my hard work was starting to pay dividends.

When getting started, I can remember chasing down a lot of realtors to work with me. Some were hard to work with. The realtors that have good production have been doing it for so long, they've already got a great relationship built with a lender. It's going to be very hard to break that up, especially when you're new to the game.

So, I focused on home builders!

Because I knew that I lived in an area with a tremendous amount of new construction going on. I did my research online and picked out all the home builders that ran right down the 10 freeway in Southern California.

I'd get up every Wednesday at 10:00 AM because that's when the sales office would be open. I'd start at the furthest builder east, and I would zig-zag my way across the freeway on the 10, hitting every home builder sales office for a stretch of about fifty miles. I'd probably finish my day somewhere around four.

I'd go into each office and talk to them for about fifty minutes, explaining the loan program that I thought was beneficial to the community based on their sales prices, home types, and the buyers in that community.

I quickly realized I had a captive audience!

Getting a realtor to take time out of their day was tough, but I knew that there was going to be a sales agent in that builder's sales office between the hours of 10 AM and 5 PM each day. So, all I had to do was walk in and be charming, start a conversation, and be consistent with that every week.

Over the course of approximately ten weeks of doing this, I built relationships, rapport, and then sooner or later someone says,

"Hey, Chris, I'm glad you showed up. The lender turned down the family for these reasons. Do you want to look at it and see if it's something you can do?"

By focusing on builders, knowing I had a captive audience, I didn't have to worry about trying to schedule them on their time and being consistent with them created a compound effect. I was becoming better at doing this job because I've seen more, I've had more repetitions and I've always tried to take that knowledge and apply it towards, growing both as a professional businessman and the business operations.

I had worked my way to branch manager at New American Funding when my friend, Nate Borghi, came to join me as the co-branch manager. Nate was one of the two friends that had pushed me to get into the mortgage business. My other good friend, Cory Tona, who also pushed me to get into the business, was with another lender working with brokers in the wholesale division. One day in 2017, Nate and I started to think about the possibility of running our own mortgage business.

We started to research,

How to start a mortgage company from the ground up?

How do you buy a mortgage company?

How do you find someone that's wanting to sell a mortgage company?

After all this research, we decided it was better to find one for sale. We needed to leapfrog a lot of the beginning steps involved in originating and closing loans fast. In 2017, we started going on a hunt looking for mortgage companies, literally cold calling owners that were doing only so much production and asking if they're interested in selling. We eventually got the right guy on the phone and came up with a plan to purchase his mortgage company.

We worked on that sales agreement through 2018, and we'd fully takeover ownership on January 1st, 2019. During this time Nate, Cory, and myself were still working other jobs preparing for this transition. We had to take all our assets to make this transaction work, to purchase this mortgage company.

We had to pay for the cost to acquire the mortgage company and put up a certain amount of collateral to be able to lend loans. At that time, collateral can be accepted in the form of cash and property. We gave as much cash as we could to the collateral, but we had to put our homes on the line. Every asset that we owned was on the line for three and a half years!

We took possession in that first year, and we're just trying to grow this business. We're having our first year of experience being owner-operators of a mortgage banking company. Big step! We roll into the first quarter, and at the end of 2019 we decided to focus on non-QM loans, specifically DSCR loans for real estate investors, which is a different type of financing.

We get past our first year; we're feeling pretty good; suddenly, we start hearing these reports of Covid, and on March 18th, 2020, the mortgage industry shuts down. We had to shut down both warehouse and product lines. The one thing we built this company on was non-QM DSCR loans and overnight gone, you can't originate or fund them!

We had to pivot and bring QM loans, conventional FHA, VA loans, which was on our planner, but probably for year three or four, but move that plan into year two, get that tuned up and live right away so the company could continue to earn revenue and not shut down.

And remember, our houses are on the line at this point!

We make it through a tough 2020 just scrapping everywhere we can. The market starts to return and we're heading into 2021 with momentum...

And, that momentum was fantastic!

In 2021 we funded 2.8 billion in loans. We saw a 21000% increase in growth year over year. That same year we were the number one growth company in lending in California. Nationally, the Inc. 500 named us the eleventh largest growing real estate company in 2021.

2021 was a great year for us!

In fact, it was mid-2022 that we as a company had gotten to a liquidity amount or a reserve amount on our balance sheet to where we were able to take our personal property off the balance sheets as collateral for lending on loans. We were so happy to have accomplished this because if this thing had fallen, it would have taken everything!

But 2022 also presented our new mortgage company with more challenges.

Inflation rate hikes, housing markets start to go sideways, mortgage companies shutting down because of poor strategies. We saw companies like Sprout, FGMC Finance of America, shut their retail arm companies like the Capital, who was a fantastic non-QM lender, decide that they're just done. So here we are looking right into the eye of the storm again and we just got to get to the next round.

Don't get knocked out.

Just get to the next round.

There's always going to be a next round.

And here we are, in the first quarter of 2023 and there's some relief on the horizon from what I can see in the way the market's going with loan origination and real estate.

Now we're going into our fourth year here as owner-operators of theLender. It's been a journey and I could not see myself doing anything else because I get to come into work every day and work on building something, like my sales team.

I get to invest in them!

I love helping my team achieve their goals of growing their careers. We have one team member in Tennessee, Nathan Gort, who is just *crushin' it* now. I couldn't be happier and prouder of Nathan and honored that he is part of our team.

And that feels good...

Because of the gratification that comes with helping someone close on a home, I don't get anymore because I don't originate loans, however, I get that feeling now when working with my team and helping them succeed so they can take care of their families.

Where is theLender today?

theLender today, is standing on its own two feet. My business partners, Cory Tona, Nate Borghi, Aaron Iverson, and Shane Harris... we've built sales operations and loan programs with a company that is battle tested. Now that we have our feet underneath us, we're looking forward to the future.

We're focused on becoming a bigger recognized brand in the non-QM space for non-QM loan investors, whether it's multi-family unit investors, STR investors, or mixed-use commercial investors. And we're committed to financing programs like bank statement loans for self-employed individuals.

We recognize non-QM borrowers as being an underserved market. So, we want to be there and commit our efforts to that mission and grow those products, originations, and create a company that brings value to the real estate industry at a high level.

ABOUT CHRIS LEDWIDGE

Pioneer and Co-Founding Partner with a demonstrated track record of driving unparalleled customer service, Chris's background includes mortgage industry experience, with a focus on real estate investor loans, builder/construction loans and residential mortgages. He serves as a member of the executive team for theLender. He maintains direct responsibility for the growth and strategic direction of the consumer direct division at theLender. His commitment to excellence, professional communication, knowledge, and ability to 'think outside of the box' have consistently produced results that speak for themselves.

Website: *www.retail.theLender.com*

9 EMANUELE PANI

 "Elegance is not catching somebody's eyes; it's staying in somebody's memory."

GIORGIO ARMANI

The thing about reputation and creating a lasting business is that it's very much like the "elegance" Mr. Armani refers to in the quote above. It might not always mean doing the "catchy" thing, but if you are committed to your guests, your journey, and creating a lasting relationship based on great fundamentals of care and love for what you do, I can promise you are going to be rewarded with something much better: a lasting impression in someone's memory—a memory and experience that is so great that it will forever be used as the benchmark by which all other similar experiences will be compared to.

I wish I could tell you that I had a clear idea of what I was doing when I started my journey in real estate/vacation rentals and that everything I have created now, twelve years later, is exactly what I had envisioned. The reality is much simpler; in a sense, the only thing I was committed to achieving was a great life, and I ran with the first opportunity I was given.

When I started working as a maintenance guy at Courtside Villas in December 2010, I was eight days out of college and knew nothing about real estate and even less about what being a maintenance guy even meant. But my boss, Hanan, realized early on that I was a natural born people-pleaser who knew how to read people well and really understood how to make someone feel heard and defuse situations (yay for childhood trauma), and if you have been working in the service and hospitality industry for any length of time, you understand how important that is. As time went on, my responsibilities grew quickly. I went from being the maintenance guy who mostly worked during Shabbat and Jewish Holidays when Hanan could not pick up the phones/conduct business to becoming the main point of contact for inhouse guest to eventually becoming the manager.

In June 2012, Hanan ended up having to move back to Israel, and we ended up purchasing the management business along with some of the units. I was 22 at the time and had no idea what I was doing, had no money or credit, but I did recognize this was, as my dad calls it, a "fundamental life moment ," one of those moments that could mean everything or nothing at all. In that moment, I remembered one of my favorite quotes from one of the great philosopher of our time Marshall Mathers, aka Eminem:

If you had
One shot
Or one opportunity
To seize everything you ever wanted
In one moment
Would you capture it
Or just let it slip?

I don't know if you remember how your mind worked when you were 22, but if you were anything like me, you spent most of your time with your head in the clouds, thinking of all the ways you would improve the business. Yes, you had a lot of great ideas, but most of them did not deserve the time/effort and resources you dedicated to them. What I realized early on when making improvements to the business is that the improvement needs to be sustainable and that you must be able to maintain the improvements you make. If not, they will just make the overall experience worse. You might be asking yourself, "E, what does that have to do with building a great reputation?" Well most times, as you are starting your business, you are going to do the good old "fake it till you make it" bit which to me is meant to mean fake the confidence that comes from experience when you only have confidence that comes from learning/education. But what most people end up doing is over-selling themselves and over-promising and ultimately under-delivering on their promises, and there is nothing worse for your reputation than being known as the person who does not follow through on their word. So my first piece of advice is this: As you are building yourself (business/life/personality), weigh your words and embrace the philosophy of "I will under-promise and over-deliver" in every single interaction you have with every single guest with no expectations, and watch how you will create loyal but most importantly raving customers.

Now that we have established you can create everything you want by being exactly who you truly are, let's dive into the next great way to win customers for life. This one is going to be hard for some of you to understand, but I know you can do it. Ready?... Your guests/customers are just people, humans going through their own unique human experience that as far as they are concerned is 100% focused on them and their hopes/dreams and fears, and you are most likely just going to be a passing blip in their journey. But what if I can tell you there is a way to make yourself memorable? Make yourself standout? I remember five or six years ago in the middle of our busy season (November to April is high season for us in South Florida, and we get a lot of snowbirds also known as cranky old people trying to escape the winter) and my onsite manager Beto calls me, "Boss, we have a lady in 10350 B, and I don't know what to do. Everything is good. The place is cleaned, but she's just complaining and yelling at me and the cleaning. She said she wants to talk to you immediately." If you already are a STR operator, you know that's the kind of phone call you never want to receive. When I first started in the business, I would take those calls so personally, almost like an insult to me and my entire team and all the hard work we do. They were times I would get so mad I was visibly shaking and my voice would crack, overall just a hot mess. But what I realized overtime is that when a guest has such an intense reaction to something and you and your team did your job to the best of your abilities, all that person wants is to be heard. When I walked in the unit with Beto to talk to the guest, I clearly remember husband quietly sitting on the couch, reading the newspaper as the wife walked out of the room, face tomato-red. Before she could say anything, I said, "Good morning, ma'am. You must be the guest that is terrorizing my staff. I grew up with an extremely picky and OCD Italian mother so you don't really scare me... what can we do to make your stay more enjoyable?" There were a few moments of silence followed by the husband laughing hysterically and smacking his knee: "C'mon, Sharyl, just tell the young man what you need. I'm sure they will take care of it." That couple just booked a unit for January and February 2023 from us and has come down every year (except during the Covid pandemic) since that first interaction. So here is advice number two: difficult people know they are difficult. When you are able to remember that their reactions are much more a reflection of how they feel about themselves vs how they feel about you and you can still show them kindness, love and deliver a great service and experience with a smile, they will never forget it. Once again, they will always compare how you made them feel when they knew they were difficult to how everyone else normally treats them.

So far, we have touched on two things: 1) Under-promise and over-deliver. 2) Remember, customers are people. I already know that if you focus on these two things, you can create a massively successful and sustainable business. I want to touch on one more thing, especially for my wanna-be real estate investors. There is a great amount of responsibility that comes with having people live in your properties, whether long term or a short term, and you have to take pride in that and not cut corners. There must be a fair exchange of value between the rate you are charging and the quality of materials/furniture you are offering your guests. The reason for that is two folds:

- If you want your business to be sustainable and fund the life of your dreams, your customers/guest must feel they are getting a fair exchange for their hard-earned money. There is no faster way to lose a customer than making them feel as if you are taking advantage of them by providing them with less than what they had expected or just a straight up bad experience.
- You must invest a part of the money you make back into creating value or adding value to your experience for your guests/customers. That will show your recurring customers that you not only care about your business but about them and about their experience/feedback too and that you are committed to your business and its longevity. There were many times early in our business that my wife Tasha and I did not have much money in the bank but always continued to invest in making the business better and better because we knew long term that was the right thing to do.

I have been extremely blessed these past few years to be the co-host of the STR Secrets podcast with my brother from another mamma Mike Sjogren. At the end of every show, we ask our guest, "What's the number one secret for success in short-term rentals?" Many people talk about the systems they use and how they can get back a lot of time or quit their jobs by leveraging technology and get to spend most of their time with family while making the same amount of money, if not more, which is honestly one of my favorite things about our industry. But when I look at what the people that have built massive businesses talk about, I can't help but realize that as much as the systems and tech you use are important, who you are, what your vision is, how you treat people and the values you stand for in running your business and life is really what makes all the difference in creating a business and a reputation that will pull you towards the highest levels of success.

Some final words to wrap up the chapter. First of all, if you are still reading this, I'm grateful to you, and I'm proud of you for all the work you are putting in to changing your current reality. Fall in love with the process of creating the life of your dreams and the inevitable up and downs of the journey. Tasha and I have a saying when shit gets a little rough: "The universe is rigged in our favor." Every single thing that happens to you happens for you, never to you. So in creating the life of your dreams, focus on that and realize a great life is not built on 100% great days, the same way a great reputation is not built on 100% five-star reviews, but on focusing on being 1% better every day and showing up by doing the things you know are right even when you don't feel like. Then all that is left is to just sit back and enjoy the blossoming of your vision.

ABOUT EMANUELE PANI

Emanuele Pani (E) was born and raised in Sardinia, Italy, and came to America at 15 to fulfill his American dream. He is a real estate expert and entrepreneur with experience in investments, real estate sales and acquisitions, and professional Airbnb hosting and management. Along with his wife Natasha, he founded Dolce Vita Vacation Rentals, a South Florida STR management company that helps families and investors create their version of the sweet life (La Dolce Vita) by finding/launching and running their STR properties. He's the co-host of the STR Secrets, a podcast that focuses exclusively on the short-term rental industry, and is a partner in Domu Private Investments, a rapidly growing investment group that focuses on investing in multifamily assets across the Southeast. In his free time, Emanuele enjoys traveling, reading/learning, cooking, working out, and spending time with his wife and pets.

Linktr.ee: *www.linktr.ee/epani*

10   KAREN CHENAILLE

If you are reading this book, you are no doubt looking for **insight and inspiration toward what it takes to build a shining reputation.** In my experience, it takes trust and tenacity. Trust in thyself to listen to your inner guidance system and tenacity to roll with the punches life will most certainly throw at you. Reputation is a paradoxical intangible asset. On one hand, you cannot directly assign a monetary value to a shining reputation; on the other, you can no doubt feel the excruciating personal and financial effects of a reputation that has not been carefully curated.

As a short-term rental operator/investor, realtor, and syndicator, I am fortunate and grateful for the guests, clients, and investors who took a chance on me solely based on what they heard through social media, podcasts or word of mouth. However, it hasn't always been this way. In 1998, I started as a W-2 employee and worked for a multitude of Fortune 500 defense contractors until 2021. During my two-decade stint in the W2 world, I came to feel that having a 'good' reputation merely meant more opportunities for greater levels of responsibility and more hours at the office all for the same pay and seemingly little recognition. I am deeply ashamed to say it now, but there were times that I intentionally underperformed to rail against the corporate system. My inner guidance system told me there had to be a better, more aligned path to abundant living.

I was raised by a single father and spent much of my childhood wearing ill-fitting Sears and Roebuck boys' Rough Neck pants because Dad felt they were a good value. Dad had very little appreciation for pre-teen fashion. I was endlessly teased and bullied in grade school. I transferred to a different school at the start of eighth grade and just never managed to fit in. Throughout my high school career, I felt like an outcast. It wasn't until I joined the Army and was trained as a Chinese linguist that I started to incubate the confidence and self-assuredness that are the hallmarks of my reputation. The military is a fantastic confidence builder, and I owe so much of who I am today to the drill sergeants and NCOs that molded and mentored me during my formative years in the military.

When I showed up for basic at the age of twenty-one, I was an unknown quantity. My high school and college achievements did not matter one iota. None of the drill sergeants knew anything about me. At that moment, I decided I wanted them to know me for my loyalty, tenacity, and intellect. As basic training progressed, my sense of *agency* became stronger, and I tenaciously held steadfast to the reputation I was developing for myself. My journey since leaving my W-2 job has been no different. When I struck out into full-time entrepreneurship in May of 2021, I had little street credibility as a realtor or investor. But I was certain of one thing: I knew my calling was helping others achieve financial independence through real estate. Despite having the knowledge and skills, I still lacked the network and gravitas to gain an audience, much less clients. I resolved to rebuild my entire reputation and engage in some serious networking to build a client base that would financially sustain me.

The financial freedom I now enjoy boils down to one thing: the reputation I built either directly by helping investor clients find cash-flowing STRs or indirectly through the reviews guests leave on short-term rental booking platforms, or the Google Reviews customers leave on our coffee shop. There is nothing special or unique about how I did this—it was a basic formula of trusting in my inner guidance system and tenaciously following the process I established to build up my reputation. You too can build up a reputation that will financially sustain you! The decision to read the inspiring stories in this book is a pivotal first step. Don't feel you have to go it alone. Find your tribe! Reach out, network, and collaborate to build a reputation you can be proud of.

ABOUT KAREN CHENAILLE

Karen is an omnipreneur living her best life in the Great Smoky Mountains of Tennessee. She and her husband Scott have five adult children and two grandchildren. Together, they operate five family-based businesses including a short term rental-focused real estate sales company, Black Sheep Realty (*www.blacksheeprealty.co*); a cozy coffee shop, The Heavenly Roast (*www.theheavenlyroast.com*); four luxury short term rentals, Star Gazer Stays (*www.stargazerstays.com*), a short term rental styling and setup business, The Best BnB Host (*www.thebest-bnbhost.com*) and a Glampground located just outside the Great Smoky Mountains National Park (*www.stargazerstaysglamping.com*).

Karen is a general partner in the Accelerate Capital Partners' short term rental syndication. Prior to becoming a full-time omnipreneur, Karen served over twenty years in corporate America and five years in the US Army as a Chinese linguist.

Website: *www.blacksheeprealty.co*

11 KYLE STANLEY

T he room could not have been much bigger than 15' x 15', but a hundred people crammed in there for a real estate MeetUp group. I was one of them, and I heard something that night that would change my life. I just didn't know it then.

 "Tell the world what you are doing and ask for nothing in return. Give away your value for free. This is what an abundance mindset is. This is what I did and what I attribute most to my success. Do this, and I'm telling you, everything will come back to you tenfold."

JASON PRITCHARD (REAL ESTATE INVESTOR IN
FRESNO, CALIFORNIA)

This one simple idea helped me create a multi seven-figure short-term rental business and two more businesses that are on pace to do seven figures in the next twelve months. I've done all of this less than three years after being in a room where I first heard Jason Pritchard speak these words.

Before I dive into this life-changing mindset, it's important to know that I struggled for over nine years to even get within reaching distance of a six-figure income, let alone seven figures.

In 2010, I came out of college in California at the ripe age of twenty-two with stars in my eyes. I believed I was going to one day be the next big ESPN sports anchor, and maybe even Chicago Cubs play-by-play broadcaster. I spent four years of college honing my broadcasting skills, only to find out that no one revealed the harsh reality of this business. I learned that most broadcast students want a position as a radio voice or TV personality for a pro team, and I was no different from the other 300+ candidates for the handful of positions that were even open to the public.

I was jobless and about to graduate in the middle of a recession, and honestly... I was freaking out. So, when my internship director told me he had a hookup for a local TV sports job for the NBC station in Grand Junction, Colorado, I didn't hesitate. I was so desperate for a job; I didn't even stop to ask what in the world Grand Junction was. I took the position, knowing just how blessed I was to even have a job offer straight out of college.

But recession or no recession, a $19, 500 salary for a full-time job was not exactly ideal. Oh, and if it took you over forty hours per week to get the job done, don't ask for overtime. If you do, they had applications from another 100+ candidates dying to replace you, and they would gladly take less than minimum wage. And if you are looking for a pat on the back, you're in the wrong place. I soon realized that it was kind of like being an umpire or referee—if your boss wasn't yelling at you, it probably meant you were doing a good job.

This once-fantasized-dream-job now felt like nothing more than a sweat factory.

I tell you this story because this was one of the first big moments of my early career. At that moment, I recognized that it was not about the industry; it was about the lifestyle. Who cares if I work in sports? If I hate the job and can't even afford to pay my bills, am I going to be truly happy? If I wanted to truly be happy, I had to build a career around the lifestyle I wanted.

Enter stage right: Kyle Stanley, the entrepreneur.

In 2011, while still working in the news, I started a business making recruiting videos for high school athletes on my days off. I built it up to about $2,000 per month, and that was enough to exceed my pitiful salary in the news. Less than two years after starting my career as a sports anchor, I was quitting to start the uncertain path of entrepreneurship.

And to be honest, this is when things got even worse. As I write this, it feels like this should be the part of the story where the hero is supposed to achieve success and leave the past in his dust while he soars to the top. Unfortunately, that is not how this story goes.

Long story short, I had created a service-based business that had a very low ceiling and called for a ton of my time. I was making a little more than I was as a sports anchor, but if you looked at my dollars per hour, I was making less!

This started another seven years of struggles, debt, ego-driven poor decisions, and plenty of alcohol to escape my true reality—my finances were spiraling out of control with no end in sight.

Fast forward to 2015: I was in the middle of a workday at home in Tempe, Arizona, when I had a moment of realization. It was 2 p.m.; I had just gone through a list of cold calls that yielded absolutely nothing, my bank account was almost empty, and I had no idea how I was going to pay my mortgage that month. I was staring out the window feeling completely helpless when I realized: I think this is rock bottom.

Now, I'm pretty blessed to say that rock bottom for me wasn't at the bottom of a bottle, drugs, crime, or anything that could do long-term damage to my reputation, but it still sucked.

In my position, rock bottom felt like failure, loneliness, desperation, emptiness, disgust, shame... the list goes on. But it was that moment of recognizing all of these feelings that things changed.

At that moment, I did what any Christian man who hadn't been to church in years would do... I prayed.

If you aren't a believer, that's okay. But this was a very important part of this story for me.

I prayed silently: "God, whatever I'm doing, it isn't working. What I'm doing is probably making things worse. I need to stop getting in your way. Tell me what to do. I give this all up to you."

Immediately, my stress, anxiety, and uncertainty left my body. This was a feeling like no other I had ever experienced. Imagine a car tire pinning you to the ground, and then it's lifted off of you without a soul in sight. You have no idea how your life was just saved, but all you know is that you have been given another chance. That was how I felt. Slightly confused, mainly relieved, but I still had no idea what the next move was.

A month later, my dad (who had been winning a twenty-year battle with prostate cancer) was diagnosed with bone cancer and given around four years to live. It was pretty clear what I needed to do next—move back home to California.

As soon as I moved back, I felt a shift. My financial situation improved, my mindset improved, and most importantly, I was reminded of how important my time was. Seeing my dad's mind and body slowly go downhill for the next few years truly made me examine what was most important in my life.

I knew I needed to create true passive income so I could buy back my time. At this point in my career, I had been trying my hand in multi-level marketing, and doing pretty well. But it was anything but passive, so I turned my attention to the most common passive income that I knew of: real estate.

With the help of some experts and a real estate education company, I got my real estate career started.

I began by flipping houses, and I even launched a podcast and YouTube channel in that first year. No, it wasn't to teach people how to flip houses. It was strictly just to connect with more expert real estate professionals. This in itself is a powerful piece of advice. Find your strengths and find a way to use them to connect yourself with the type of people you want to emulate. For me, that was podcasting. If you are good at writing, start a blog. If you are good at numbers, offer to analyze deals. If you are good at marketing, offer to help them get their name out there. There are tons of ways to bring value to people. Find your way and use it as your conversation starter.

Anyway, back to the story.

After flipping my first house a couple of months in, I got my next deal. It was my first shot at passive income. I bought a house that was going to net me $600 per month as a long-term rental. I was stoked!

And during the renovation process, a voice inside hit me with a question that would change my life: "What if I did this as a short-term rental instead?"

No way. That wouldn't work, right? Who would want to come to Fresno, California? We aren't a vacation spot.

But I looked it up on Airbnb, and there were over 150 short-term rentals in Fresno. And they were booked! Almost all of them! I couldn't believe it.

I talked to a mentor (John) and told him what I was planning to do. His thoughts were much like mine. He didn't believe it would work but said to let him know if it worked (insert very obvious foreshadowing).

In month one, I listed it on Airbnb. Here were the exact numbers:

Income: $4,240.06
Mortgage: $1,283
Utilities: $408
Cleaning: $500
Total Net Profit: $2,048.94

In one month, I 3.5 X'd my income compared to a long-term rental. Are you kidding me? I struck gold! And I wanted to do it again and fast.

That's when I learned how I could do this without even owning the house. Once again, I decided to skip the heartache of trying to learn through mistakes, and I found someone who was already great at this, and I bought his course and got to work.

I couldn't believe it, but the model worked! In six months, I had six properties live on Airbnb, and I was netting just shy of $8,000.

But here's the worst part: no one knew. I had a secret, and I wasn't even close to letting it out. I had a scarcity mindset.

Skip ahead a couple months, there I was, in that 15' x 15' room. Shoulder to shoulder with investors. And that's when I heard Jason Pritchard challenge my mindset. It was as if he was speaking to me only.

"Tell the world what you are doing and ask for nothing in return. Give away your value for free. This is what an abundance mindset is. This is what I did and what I attribute most to my success. Do this, and I'm telling you, everything will come back to you tenfold."

Internal voice: "There's way more potential for competition with what I'm doing. That doesn't apply to me."

And as I found out pretty quickly, all of these excuses were wrong...

The first time I talked about Airbnb was on my podcast, The Fearless Investor, which at the time was called Fearless Flipping. I casually mentioned that I had a few Airbnbs. It was a passing comment during an interview. The guest not only asked about it, but I had people from my audience reaching out directly to me asking to learn more about Airbnb.

Internal voice: "Crap, maybe this abundance mindset thing works."

So, I got a little more intentional about it.

At the next local MeetUp group, I started telling people what I was doing. I got similar responses:

"Tell me more about that."

"That's working for you in Fresno?"

"I'd love to take you to lunch and pick your brain about that."

It was very obvious that I was doing something that everyone was interested in.

I took the abundance mindset one step further...

I started a Facebook group. Then I invited people to book calls with me to learn more about Airbnb. Then I offered to teach people how to start their first Airbnb listing.

Before I knew it, I had over 1,000 members in my Facebook group, my YouTube channel and podcast started to gain more traction, and I was making money by teaching people the business.

But the real fun happened when my mentor and I reconnected about Airbnb. As I mentioned before, he wanted me to keep him updated on how things were going. When I finally told him, he offered me one of his houses, but he wanted to furnish it and wanted me to manage it for a fee.

It was a new opportunity, and it came because I was trying out this whole abundance mindset thing.

I crunched the numbers, and I was blown away. With this house, we both could net over $1,000 per month!

In fact, after a bit of research, it turned out other people were already doing this. They even had a name for it: "Co-Hosting."

I signed my second co-hosting deal quickly after that, and it felt like I was about to turn this thing into something big.

Only one issue: it was March 2020 (cue the depressing music).

Yup. COVID-19 hit, and the sky was falling. Or so it felt. I paused five of my eight Airbnbs and started doing month-to-month tenants. It seemed like the most logical move.

But this crazy thing happened. My three Airbnbs kept getting booked. From March until June, I was 90% occupied at great rates. How was this possible? I thought everyone was scared to breathe the outside air.

And of course, everyone wanted to know how Airbnb was doing during this pandemic.

Internal voice: "Tell them it's struggling. Scare them away. That way, you can make more money and have less competition."

It was tough to ignore that voice. That was my instinct! But I knew I needed to stick with this new voice. The abundance voice. So I told everyone just how well it was doing.

And of course, it proved to be the right move again.

From July to November 2020, we went from eight units to twenty-five units, all with other people's properties. That's four months and seventeen new units. Each makes us close to $1,000 each.

In November, I made just south of $23,000. That more than doubled my largest month in anything I had ever done. And may I remind you, that was $3,500 more than my first full-time job in the news paid me in an entire year!

In May 2021, we added more listings, and I made $33,000. July 2021: $42,000, December 2021: $55,000. And today as I write this, not only have we had multiple months of earning over $65,000 with our Airbnb portfolio, but we have also had months where we have earned more than $50,000 from educating others in this industry.

Had I not taken Jason Pritchard's advice in 2019, I'm completely convinced that I would have maybe fifteen to twenty Airbnbs, and I would still be flipping the occasional house on the side. Not a bad life. After expenses, I'd probably be making around $15K to $20K per month. But nowhere close to where I am now.

But because I bought into the abundance mindset, I opened doors that I never knew were possible. I've met entrepreneurs that I never would have known existed. I've helped people that I would have never known needed the help. Heck, I probably even met my wife because of it (we met on Facebook and started talking because we were both in real estate). And I'm able to do it all while still having a business that complements my ideal lifestyle.

It's a funny thing. After this lightbulb moment in 2019, I am now able to see it so clearly. All of the people who I have tried to emulate have had this abundance mindset.

John, my mentor that I mentioned earlier, took me under his wing and asked for nothing in return. He's one of the most successful people I know. He could have easily told me to kick rocks, but he chose to help me. But you know who I thought of when I had deals that I couldn't take on by myself? John.

My wife and I have two amazing friends, Erin and Cleadus, who flip luxury houses here in Fresno. They make amazing money doing it, and they are always so giving. Whether it's with their time, their money, their knowledge, or their deals. They are always giving. And you know who people think of when they want to get into flipping luxury houses? Erin and Cleadus.

Of course Jason Pritchard. He doesn't just talk the talk; he walks the walk. He openly educates hundreds of people at his MeetUp groups and asks for nothing in return. But you know who people think of when they have a deal and don't know what to do with it? Jason.

And now every time someone says the word "Airbnb," most people in my town think of me. I bought into the abundance mindset, and it delivered. I have so many deals coming to me that I now have to turn most of them away! That would not have happened if I wasn't giving away free information every day.

And I even give free information out to the world. If you want to learn more from me, I encourage you to check out all of my free content on my website: *www.fearlesskyle.com.* You can get connected to my YouTube channel and podcast from there as well.

But more importantly, buy into the abundance mindset. Find a way today to give value away for free and ask for nothing in return.

ABOUT KYLE STANLEY

Kyle Stanley is a short-term rental investor and manager out of Fresno, CA. In 2019, Kyle learned he could operate short-term rentals in homes that he didn't own, and that's when he realized he could scale the business quickly. In under three years, Kyle went from zero to sixty-five listings, grossing over $3 million per year. He has also built a team that has completely automated the day-to-day management for him. With the extra time, he now teaches others how to replicate his path.

> ***Website:*** *www.fearlesskyle.com*
> ***Facebook:*** *www.facebook.com/groups/airbnbmasterminds*
> ***YouTube:*** *www.bit.ly/fearlessinvestor*

12 MICHAEL HICKS

My real estate career began at an early age. Albeit a slow start and progression, it was a start. I was fortunate enough to grow up around some pretty solid individuals, individuals who set amazing examples for a young man getting started in the real estate business. One of those happened to be a developer by the name of Jimmy H "Wink" Baker. Wink was my best friend's dad way back in middle school. He would purchase large tracts of land and break it up into lots for builders to come in and build new homes. Wink would often times pick us up from school and take us fishing in the evenings but not before dropping by a job site to check on progress or drop off needed materials for the subcontractors. I was always intrigued by the process and asked many questions along the way. As a twelve/thirteen-year-old, Wink's ability to be on the move and so flexible with his schedule always stood out to me. I was used to seeing my dad work from seven to four with scheduled days off so having the freedom to head to the lake in the middle of the week definitely piqued my interest.

I finally got an opportunity to begin working for Wink in the summers, afternoons, and weekends. It was intriguing to me to see the process of taking a vacant piece of land, clearing, grading, adding utilities, subdividing, and eventually building homes on these once wooded and unde-veloped lots. I later found that I really enjoyed seeing a pile of lumber turn into a home as well. The days were long and hot. As the subdivisions were coming to completion, the roads were paved and concrete curbs were added to give it the finishing touch. The dozer would then come along, pushing the dirt from the yards up against the newly poured curbs, causing some of the dirt to spill over into the roads. I, along with a few other middle schoolers, walked the miles of new roads, where we would shovel the dirt from the roads back into the lots. Then the fun work began. The freshly graded lots had to be covered with seed and straw to prepare for grass, which involved walking the miles of roads again, sowing grass and spreading thousands of bales of wheat straw. If you've never done this, you'll know it's no fun. Especially at $5 an hour. It taught me work ethic. A work ethic that most twelve-to-thirteen-year-olds didn't know. Wink would smile and say there's dependable Michael as I arrived to work and my friends did not. That stuck with me!

While Wink gave me the opportunity to work and learn, my parents were also a big influence on my growth as a young man, teaching me the importance of being on time and putting in an honest day's work, doing what you said you would do, when you said you would do it, and like my dad always said, "can't never could do it."

During the same time I was working for Wink, my parents helped me purchase a push mower so that I could begin mowing yards while I wasn't working elsewhere. I didn't realize it then but it was a bigger commitment for them at the time than it was for me. They were the ones who had to drive me to wherever it was I was cutting yards. They guided me in the right directions and made sure that I was around good solid people who did things the right way, with honesty and integrity. They were also instrumental in me achieving my rank as Eagle Scout, making sure I was at meetings and completing the ranks necessary to advance through scouting where the scout oath taught us to help others at all times, to keep myself physically strong, mentally awake, and morally straight. I was also active in the Key Club, which taught us to build our home, school, and community. I have strived to keep these principles throughout my life and live them out to the best of my ability, passing them down to my children in the process. Back to my parents… they were also a big influence in my move into real estate. I watched from the sidelines as they purchased rentals here and there, rehabbed and sold a house here and there, and I helped them clean up a few properties as well. I remember begging them to let me buy a couple mobile home lots when I was sixteen as I had been saving money for a while and could have figured out a way, or at least I felt that way. They said no and that there would be plenty more opportunities for me to purchase in the future. I replied "That's not fair and there won't be any good deals left." We laugh about that now as they remind me almost every time I purchase another "good deal."

Growing up, we had things that most of my friends didn't have. We had a nice house, a pool, a few acres and many cool toys like an elevated playhouse, zipline, a BMX track in the woods, and a batting cage with a mechanical pitching machine to name a few. I constantly heard snide remarks from my friends that we were rich and the likes, which bothered me because I knew that was far from the truth. I remember many occasions where we ate pinto beans for several days at a time when there was more month than there was money. My dad worked hard so that my mom could stay home with us kids and take care of things around the house. We were so blessed to have her home with us as she was always teaching us something…which could be a little annoying at times but hey, I can still recite my prepositions! As I grew older, I learned that my parents hand dug the swimming pool and installed it themselves. They built their own house. My dad would carry shingles up on the roof during the day and my mom would nail them on while he was delivering mail at the post office. The pitching machine was about to be thrown away by the parks department, and he was able to fix it. He traded an old trailer frame to a guy with a bulldozer to build the BMX track. I can't remember where our playhouse came from but it was a trade of some type. Turns out the playhouse was a really large doghouse that my dad lifted up and placed on stilts (telephone poles he had collected), adding a deck, fireman pole, and slide. All from salvaged materials. There are so many lessons to be taken from my parents, and I am sure there are many more of these instances that I am not aware of, but it taught me that you have to put in the work to make your dreams become a reality. To this day, I still struggle not being active in our new construction projects. I have a desire to be hands on. Their actions taught me the art of trade and barter, that other things had value, not just money. That you can add value to something by being able to make the repairs or "fix it up." And most importantly, to be creative in your endeavors. How many kids did you know growing up that had a treehouse built from a repurposed doghouse fully equipped with a slide, fireman's pole, and zip line built by the coolest parents ever? Drive and work ethic made this possible. Even in her mid-seventies, she will still outwork me and most anyone I know.

Fast forward a few years, I had graduated high school and left for college...because that's what I was expected to do. I pushed through a whole semester and a half and knew that the college route was not for me. I couldn't stand the thought or should I say it pained me to have to sit through an archery class in order to achieve a degree in Business Management (Even though I enjoyed the archery). I just knew that I could be doing something more productive with my time and my life.

So, half way through my second semester, I came home and visited my developer friend Wink. Just like my parents, he wasn't very excited about me leaving college. I came to him with the idea that I wanted to build a house...and he didn't laugh. Thankfully he believed in me and was willing to help me through the process. At the time, I had been around construction and been through trade classes in high school, which gave me a lot of general ideas but I for sure didn't know how to build a house. Wink placed the lot in my name and created a zero interest one-year note, using the lot as collateral. In order for me to go to the bank and get a loan, I needed some skin in the game. This is where the lot came in. Remember that note that Wink prepared? He didn't record it. This enabled me to go to the bank and use the lot as collateral to obtain the construction loan I needed to build the home. So, at the age of nineteen, I built my first home and never looked back. A lot of lessons came from this first project. Creative deal structuring, seller financing, and that I was capable of hard things.

You see, through the years when Wink called me to come and work, I showed up when I said I would. I worked hard and stayed until the work was done while a lot of the other guys my age would either not show up or leave half way through the day. I had proven to Wink over the years that I was dependable and trustworthy. My parents taught me from a young age that a man is only as good as his word. This was usually prefaced by "your grandpa always said." My grandpa passed away when I was seven and something about that preface made me even prouder of my name, giving me a sense of pride and a sense of not wanting to let my grandpa down. For years after my grandpa's death, I heard stories of the kind of man he was. I never wanted to let him down or anyone else for that matter. My parents taught me that you can replace almost anything in life except your name. You're given one name and you develop a reputation that goes along with that name. Once you tarnish that name, there's little that can be done to undo the damage. Do what you say you're going to do, when you say you're going to do it. That's the long way around of telling you how I got started in real estate and there's so much that went on from then until now. I felt it was necessary as I really struggled with how the reputation piece played into my business as it's just something that was engrained in me from an early age and has remained consistent throughout my business and personal life.

Shortly after the new construction project, I acquired my first two single family rentals. I formed my comparable property list by spending hours studying the classified ads in the newspaper, correlating prices with neighborhoods in my area so that I could have an accurate offer when the time came. When I say I had spent hours, it was every Sunday afternoon from the age of sixteen to nineteen. I would sit on the couch with a highlighter, marking the properties that I felt I could afford and then asking my dad what he thought about them. Being a mailman, my dad knew the areas I was searching pretty well. He would usually respond with "that's in a flood plain" or "those are really steep lots" or "the houses in that neighborhood are really rundown." I felt like the first property would never come but it finally did in the form of a HUD home. This long process taught me patience and diligence.

The second, a seller financed home from the next-door neighbor shortly after the first. This was early 2000s, before Bigger Pockets, before real estate meetups, and before YouTube so any information I gathered was through reading books and talking to those in my small circle who had a couple of rentals. Mistakes were made, rehabs were underestimated, and rents barely covered the expenses but I took action. I was not willing to give up on the idea that I could create a retirement through real estate. I had big plans and this was my path to get there.

Over the next twenty years, we were able to add more long term rentals, commercial warehousing, self-storage facilities, and finally short term rentals to our portfolio mix. While I had no idea where this real estate path would take me, I never imagined that it would be the means to an end of a w2 job. I had no idea the number of amazing people that it would put me in front of over time. It was just a side hustle and a way to provide for myself and my family.

Along the way, I met individuals who would alter the course of mine and my family's lives. The first was Charlie. I found Charlie when my back was against the wall, three properties under contract, and a partner that just dropped out of funding those three properties. Charlie is one of those guys that have a lot to say. After building over 7000 units and developing over 400 subdivisions, he has the right to say it! One of those people that when they are speaking, you need to listen. We've worked well together, and he has become a great friend, mentor, and private lender to me, never being afraid to let me know if he thought I was walking into a bad investment and always there to encourage and advise. Being around him has always been uplifting and made me reach higher in my goals. He gave me the confidence to go further than I had ever imagined.

Bill Cook is another individual who has played a large role in shaping my real estate investment career. Bill is just one of those guys that I knew I wanted to be around from the moment I first heard him speak. He brings to the table a unique way of structuring deals and making things work where others cannot. This is where it all came together for me. Bringing together everything I had learned and putting it together in a manner that I was familiar with. Remember when I talked about my dad bartering and producing things that most never had? Now I could couple one of the things I loved most (bringing value other than money) to real estate. This was pure magic and this is also when my investing really took off. I had a complete mindset shift and no longer felt that I was at the mercy of the banks. Seller financing with no money down, no interest, no payments for x number of months, and the list goes on and on. The possibilities were endless now. There is not a time that I sit down with Bill that I don't learn something new or hear something that makes me ponder life's many choices and decisions. He taught me that there is no box. So, stop trying to think outside of one.

Once I took on the mindset of not having a box, I had a whole new outlook on investing. Being a creative person, what had once been exciting, building and flipping houses, was now a bore, and I really did not enjoy these things anymore. They had become mundane and were no longer challenging to me individually. They were more of a chore, and I could no longer get excited. It was a mere process. Same flooring, same countertops, cabinets, trim, paint, the list goes on and on. I hated it! This is what led me into the short-term rental industry.

When I say short-term rentals, it's probably not what you think. While they are short-term rentals, we did them with a bit of a twist. We began building shipping container homes, treehouses, and a-frames. These things had been done so we figured we'd take it a step further. What's the number one rule in real estate? Location, location, location! We couldn't build these unique structures and then throw them on any old ordinary lot. We had to find THE lots! This led us to buying premium lots that were waterfront or had amazing long mountain range views, which created experiences seldom found in the short-term rental world. We have now built a brand around these unique properties and will settle for nothing less than these standards.

Who knows where our investing career will take us next? What I do know is that because of the amazing people I surround myself with, I will continue to grow and will always be adapting, taking the traits that I have picked up from those individuals and doing business the right way. Remember, while your reputation is important, it's subjective. Three different people will have three different opinions of your reputation based on their perception, which is based more on their life circumstances than yours. What they can't take away is your character.

I'm so thankful for all of the friends I've made along the way. There are so many that keep me in line and push me to do more. My parents, Teah, Ryan, Jay, Joey, Kerry, Randy, Adrian, Bill, Wink, Charlie, Elizabeth, Sarah, Annette, Amy, Wendy, Tanya, Stacey, Miranda, Kylan, Chelsea, Mr. Wilson, Steve, my scout leaders, and my Key Club Family. Thank you for molding me into the man I am today. I am forever grateful.

Surround yourself with those will make you better, those who hold you accountable, and those who encourage you.

ABOUT MICHAEL HICKS

Michael has over twenty years of experience in residential and commercial real estate ranging from single family homes, multi-family, commercial warehousing, and self-storage. With just under 300 deals under his belt, Michael began his career in new construction and is still building homes today. Just a little differently. In 2016, Michael and wife Teah moved into short-term rentals by converting one of their duplexes. They never looked back and began building unique short-term rentals in 2020. Their homes have been viewed over five million times on various social media platforms, been featured in multiple magazines and A & E's Living Smaller TV Series. Shipping Container Homes, Tree-houses, and A-Frames so far and they're just getting started.

Website: www.wanderchatt.com
Linktr.ee: www.linktr.ee/findyourrepurpose

13 MICHELLE SCHWEINSBURG

All things Real Estate and being a mom are among the top things I enjoy most in life right now.

As a young adult, right out of college, I started strategically planning my career path and future goals so that they would align with being a mother one day. I had no idea when that "one day" would be, but I estimated it to be at least a decade away. However, even with that milestone being so far in the future I knew that I always wanted to be a present, hands-on type of mom. I wanted to make sure that I had flexibility and control over my work schedule to ensure I could attend PTA meetings, coach little league, attend school field trips, etc.

So...I went into Corporate Regional Sales and built a very solid, successful career over the next twelve years and eventually went on to get my Master's Degree in Hospitality Management. This career path gave me flexibility with my time and was financially sound.

However, it still didn't give me the type of schedule autonomy I knew I would need and desire when I became a mom. A core belief of mine back then, which still holds even more true today, is that life is meant to be lived and experienced, not to simply exist and work your life away at a job where you are ultimately disposable.

I decided that I needed to create my own career path and began to start thinking about real estate as a profession and business opportunity. I had always been interested in homes, their architecture and interior design, and I had dabbled in investing as a house hacker and had owned several homes. In 2016 I decided to get my real estate license in Florida and learn the industry as a realtor while still working my Corporate Sales role. My plan was to get experience and build up a reputation and referral network over the next few years so that I could sustain myself solely on selling real estate. This is what I did for several years.

Then in 2018, I found out I was finally going to be a mom! This news changed my life path in many ways that I didn't even consider at the time. As we were beginning to prepare for our new baby, we decided we needed a bigger home and wanted to move to a suburban community. However, we had a cute two-bedroom beach bungalow with a pool in South Florida, and I just had a FEELING this home would do great on Airbnb. But remember this was back in 2018 before it was super popular and before anyone was using AirDNA or before STR deal tools even existed; so this was based more on a gut feeling. The next hurdle was going to be convincing my boyfriend to trust my instinct and to let me try renting it on Airbnb for three months. But, all we needed was two months and our eyes were WIDE OPEN at the possibility of what this property could do for us as an extra revenue stream for our family. On top of the financial benefit, I genuinely enjoyed talking to the guests that were traveling into town to stay at our home! I got to know people's stories and hear about how they made family memories in our backyard. Some would rebook each season, others would write beautiful thank-you messages. It was heart-warming and genuine. I think my hospitable nature really enjoyed the people connection part of this "hobby" at that time.

After I had my son, Beckham, in 2019 and went back to my corporate job after my maternity leave ended, I was constantly thinking about wanting to spend as much time with my new baby as possible. Shortly after that, Covid happened and I took full advantage of life slowing down and allowing me to spend my days with my son. But I also spent many of my evenings learning everything I could about buying a successful investment property with the intention of building an STR portfolio. I listened to podcasts, joined BiggerPockets, read books, joined the only STR Facebook group at the time, researched markets tirelessly, learned how to analyze a deal and spent time making connections to learn from others that were just a few steps ahead of me.

By 2021 I had purchased two more STR properties that closed within one week of each other! These properties were in two different states and both were over twelve hours away. I quickly learned in real time how to interview realtors, find reputable contractors, how to furnish properties that were 800 miles away, build a team of local cleaners and handymen, manage renovations from out of state, decorate with local culture, get professional photos taken, create an Airbnb listing, learn about dynamic pricing technology, create digital welcome guide books, and manage guest communications to launch both properties just in time for the holidays! To say it was a hectic couple of months would be an understatement especially while having a two-year-old at home and still working at my corporate job. But they were launched and came out of the gate strong.

And then a couple months later I had my ah-hah moment while up late at night binge-watching Selling Sunset. Yes, you heard that right... watching Selling Sunset; this show changed my life! The most obvious career pivot was right in front of me but it took some guilty pleasure reality tv viewing to make me slow down and think for a moment. And then it seemed so obvious...

Why don't I focus my real estate business on working with investors to help them find an STR property here in South Florida?!

It made total sense. I live in a vacation market that is very STR friendly in regards to the local regulations, I own and manage my own STR investment properties, I'm already well connected and immersed into the STR investor groups, I absolutely love talking to people about running an Airbnb, and I have contacts here for housecleaners, contractors, and handymen. This is a huge benefit to be able to help provide the infrastructure needed for an investor to expand into a new market. I decided this was the perfect combination of professional and personal experience to truly be able to help other investors find their next property to add to their portfolio. So, this is exactly what I did. I began rebranding my real estate business and decided to be laser-focused on helping both experienced and first-time STR investors find a home in the West Palm Beach and Fort Lauderdale markets. I went all in and left my corporate sales job at the end of 2021 and have not looked back!

I also was forced to quickly adapt to a fast-changing climate within the industry. As I was redefining my career it was one of the craziest times in the history of real estate with record low inventory, historically low interest rates, multiple offers being submitted well-over list price, and properties going "Under Contract" within hours of hitting the market. I am thankful to have had a solid background in the industry and a solid moral compass. During this time I saw a lot of reckless behavior amongst buyers, sellers, and agents. There were also many new investors entering the market who were eager to acquire their first STR property. And as I look back over this last year I can truly say that passion, authenticity, and integrity have been the pillars of my success and honestly the core of who I am. REPUTATION matters.

I believe when working with investors, the most important things to first understand are their goals for the property. When I first start working with a client or have an investor reach out to me, the very first thing I do is set up a call or meeting to understand their goals and their knowledge of managing STRs in general, as well as their knowledge of the South Florida region. Experienced investors may tell me they are looking for a value-add property and they are looking for appreciation opportunity as well as cash flow. Other investors may tell me this is a property that my family plans to use over the years as a vacation home or possibly their retirement home and cash flow is less important. Others may want to learn about all possible exit strategies and discover that a mid-term rental better suits their goals. New investors may need a lot of educating on why I don't recommend investing in an HOA community or how to analyze deals and utilize the tools available such as STR Insights, AirDNA, and Rabbu. Without knowing the buyers' goals you are unable to serve them properly. I have been known on a regular basis to show buyers potential properties for them that are well below their pre-approved amount from their lender. Many people, including the buyers sometimes, are surprised I would present a $600k house when they are they are pre-approved up to $2 Million. But in this market typically the cash flow or cash on cash returns are strongest for STR properties when in the range of $400-800k. The $2M house may gross similar revenue as an Airbnb as a $700k property, but clearly your ROI and cash flow will be much stronger on a $700k home thus making it a much smarter deal for an investment property with the purpose of making it a short term rental. This is why it is so valuable to find an experienced realtor who understands how investors shop differently than primary home buyers. For example, STR investors do not typically care if there are walk-in closets or if it's in a good school district; in comparison, these are often very important criteria for home buyers shopping for their personal home.

The transition into my new career was pretty seamless since I was so immersed in the STR and investing world personally and by this time I had seven years of being a realtor under my belt. However, there were still challenges to adjust to. I quickly realized that being a realtor during this time when there was a sense of urgency and scarcity for buyers that this also meant that your schedule could change seven times a day due to having to go tour properties or write offers for clients almost immediately as they hit the market. This very quickly presented a challenge in my family life because I had a three-year-old now at home and only had a part-time nanny. As I mentioned before, I always knew I wanted to be a hands-on mom and to me, that meant I did not want my son in daycare for forty to fifty hours per week. Having a part-time nanny that worked three days a week was sufficient and worked great when I had a predictable Corporate Sales job that had set days and I could schedule my meetings during the hours I had daycare.

So, my son started coming along with me to virtual showings, home inspections, and even closings on occasion. However, I was always nervous that he would be too loud or it would appear "unprofessional" to my clients. When I had to bring him along to do a virtual tour I would always bring toys or his tablet to try to occupy him for twenty minutes while I recorded the video walk-through for the buyers. But I often found myself telling him to sit quietly while mommy does this video or that he can't talk while I am filming and that he must stay out of the way. Then one day the mom guilt set in HARD. He looked sad and said "NO More Homes Mommy." And there was a moment that I realized that the very type of career I had always tried to create for when I was a mother was the exact opposite of what my child was experiencing. I struggled with this situation for a few months and interviewed other nannies and toured daycare facilities, but ultimately it landed me back on leaving my son for more hours with a stranger to raise him than I ever wanted to.

I also realized this career path did not have set work hours and sometimes I had to work in the evening or on the weekends. And that's when I thought to myself that when your professional life blends into your personal life, why should the personal life side have to be hidden?

So instead of telling my son he had to be quiet, I chose to embrace his presence when filming walk-through videos or doing virtual tours for buyers. I chose to include him and allow him to feel empowered and important, sometimes telling him that I needed his help to show a home today. I often introduce him as "my assistant" on camera and it has been extremely well received by my clients. Many have gotten to the point where they look forward to seeing Beckham being the "tour guide" in the videos and if I send them a home tour without him, they instantly ask: "where is your assistant today"? As a mom, that warms my heart more than anything when the people I am spending so much time with during their real estate transactions have taken an interest and enjoy me sharing him.

I have realized that being authentic and staying true to your values makes you relatable and humanizes the entire experience. It becomes less transactional and more about the relationship. People like to do business with people they like and trust. And I like to serve people who I like and trust. Even my home inspector has taken him under his wing because he has come along on many inspections over the years. Now he is part of my "team" and it's wonderful to be able to share the favorite part of my life with the people I work closely with while helping them change their life by finding the perfect investment property. Relationships, reputation and integrity are priceless in this industry.

The last couple years I have lived and breathed real estate and all things short term rentals. I have found a great tribe of other investors and hosts along the way. We have given each other support, advice, and mentorship, and some have even become business partners. However, I always felt like moms who owned short term rentals and self-managing them had a different group of balls in the air that they were juggling. Especially moms with young kids who aren't in school yet...which is exactly the season of life I am currently in! I see so many female investor groups (which I am also a part of), and new investor groups, and young millennial groups, but I also think there should be a Moms Investor community. So at the beginning of this year, I decided to create and launch a community called "STR Mom" myself for all the investor moms.

The vision for STR Mom is to establish a social community and resource for moms that have short term rental properties or who may be thinking of investing in one to see how it can add value to their family life and financial health. It will provide a sense of community with other women going through this same experience for all of us walking through the journey of motherhood. I hope there will be a massive connection shared and relationships formed.

There will also be tools, videos, and resources for new investors who want to see a blueprint of how to navigate the process of choosing a market, analyzing a deal, finding a realtor, furnishing a property, marketing, guest communications, automation of property management, leveraging technology, etc. All of this will be discussed and shared from my perspective of doing it with an infant or toddler. My hope is just to create a resource and community for Moms to bond and form a tribe throughout their investing journey and offer inspiration to anyone considering investing in an STR.

The best way to reach out to me or follow along on information about the South Florida STR real estate market is to find me on Facebook @STRrealtor. To join the STR Mom tribe for free please join the group on Facebook at @STRmom or go to my website at *www.STRmom.com*.

ABOUT MICHELLE SCHWEINSBURG

Michelle has been selling real estate since 2016 in the West Palm Beach and Fort Lauderdale markets in the South Florida region. She specializes in helping investors buy and sell short term rental (STR) properties for use as Airbnb vacation home rentals. Her passion, knowledge, and authenticity are a rare find within the real estate industry. Michelle also owns and self-manages her own short term rental portfolio, which spans the Mid-Atlantic and Southeast markets. She has been an Airbnb Super-Host since 2019. The hospitality industry is not new to her; prior to being a realtor, she worked for Hilton in the Corporate Sales Office. Michelle also has a Master's Degree in Hospitality Management from Old Dominion University. As an investor herself, she also offers consulting services for hosts who want to learn how to self-manage their properties and create generational wealth for their family through real estate investing. In January 2023, she launched *STR Mom*, an online community to support moms who also are investors in the short term rental space. The vision for STR Mom is to establish a social community and resource for moms that have short term rental properties or who may be thinking of investing in one to see how it can add value to their family life and financial health. It will provide a sense of community with other women going through this same season of life. Michelle has a three-year-old son named Beckham. She lives in West Palm Beach, FL, with her fiancé, Justin, and three rescue dogs. You can follow Michelle on Facebook at STR Mom and also on her business real estate page at Michelle Schweinsburg: STR Realtor of South Florida.

Website: *www.STRmom.com*

14 RYAN DUFFY

What do you do for a living?

I was asked this question at a neighborhood Christmas party a few years ago, and I wasn't really sure how to answer it. My wife Shae and I were coming into a strange transition in our professional careers. She was an interior designer and a licensed real estate agent. I was a general contractor with a home builder's license and had just passed my real estate exam. It was the end of 2019, and we had recently turned our home into a full time short term rental that we cleaned and managed ourselves.

To respond by saying I'm a Realtor, builder, host, cleaner and manager would have been a little bit of a mouthful. I can't honestly remember how I answered this question but it got me thinking about who I was professionally. What was our actual value proposition to current and future clients? What sort of image and reputation do we want to have for our business?

I've had a little while to reflect on that now and our business model has evolved from those early years. We've started a real estate brokerage licensed in Missouri and Arkansas (and likely Oklahoma by the time this story goes to print). Our firm specializes in investment real estate in the Ozarks (STR, new construction, flip and development) with in-house construction and management services. Now we have several agents, a dedicated construction crew and a full time administrative staff assisting with our real estate transactions, new construction projects and property management, which has enabled me to manage the big picture and have better control of my schedule. It took a while to get here though.

Priceless Marketing

Marketing is one of the main keys to success in the real estate industry (or any other for that matter). Starting out as new agents in a community that we had recently relocated to from 500 miles away, Shae and I really had to boot-strap our business. She did 99% of the heavy lifting early on as I was swinging a hammer to keep a steady flow of income as we got started.

Calling for sale by owner listings off of Zillow and door knocking while eight months pregnant with our second child in the July heat were two of Shae's more successful methods of lead generation. It wasn't long after the week of door knocking and phone calls that she was in labor and delivery on the phone between contractions guiding one of her first deals across the finish line. Her level of care and dedication to her clients in that deal established the foundation for something that no level of sponsored ads, billboards or paid lead service could ever buy; a reputation for being a strong negotiator and a fierce advocate for her clients. Shae not only had clients; she had raving fans. They loved her grit and genuinely wanted to see her succeed. Shae had set the bar pretty high by the time I was able to get my license and start working with her.

The Unicorn with Covid

The first listing I was able to secure was a For Sale By Owner (FSBO) I spotted on Facebook Marketplace. It looked too good to be true. It was a five-bedroom home with no short term rental restrictions on five lake-front acres being sold fully furnished with a boat slip and private swim dock for $340,000. I called it a Unicorn. This was like an elusive and mystical creature that had just walked out of the woods and stared me in the eyes. It checked the boxes for just about every investor looking in our market. This was almost impossible to find! I happened to be home with our then-two-year-old daughter Lana when I saw the post. I grabbed some snacks, strapped her in the booster seat and went off to take a look.

The seller was from out of state and his sister, who lived in the area, met me to show the house and acted more or less as his de facto agent. She lit up when I walked through the door with Lana. She had several grand-children herself and a huge dollhouse set up in the living room from when they were younger. Lana got to play while I walked through the house and took some amateur photos and videos to send to a couple of prospective clients. An hour later we were loading that dollhouse up in the car and heading home. Lana made out like a bandit on that showing.

The next day I had a full-price offer for the seller. My buyer wanted to lock this thing down quickly knowing it was underpriced. The next few weeks progressed as most other real estate deals do. I went back there a few more times to take inventory of the furniture and belongings that were going to be conveyed with the sale of the home and to take some measurements of the rooms to get an idea of remodel costs. The various inspections happened. We negotiated a few miscellaneous repairs and it seemed like smooth sailing all the way to the closing table.

I was looking forward to getting another closing under my belt. We were getting ready to start on our second investment property and it needed to be gutted, remodeled and furnished into a vacation rental. We were scraping together every penny we had as we knew this was going to be a long and expensive process. It was early March 2020.

Then it all hit the fan. I got a call from the buyer two days before closing saying that he had to back out of the deal. The market was in a freefall, he had just retired the month before and was watching his retirement fund evaporate as the economy and the world shut down for Covid. He couldn't pull the trigger on an investment property with everything that was going on. I still had him protected under a financing contingency so we got a note from his lender, presented it to the seller and recovered his earnest deposit.

This was a gut punch for everyone involved. The buyer was bummed to miss out on this opportunity. The seller had all of his personal items moved out and his sister (who had been taking care of the property) sold the riding mower that she'd been using to mow the five-acre yard. I was out a commission check that I had been looking forward to for remodel expenses and, although I was glad my buyer hadn't gotten into something that would've made him feel financially pinched, I felt for the seller.

I had just spent weeks working on this deal. I wasn't ready to let it go yet. Being an FSBO I didn't have a fiduciary responsibility to the seller and it was my job to get the best deal possible for my buyer but I ended up building a great rapport with him and his sister. I called them up and made my case to list it. They were leaving money on the table. Not being intimately familiar with the market and the level of demand for properties like this that could be used as nightly rentals, they were underpricing their property by $40,000. The reasoning behind not wanting to list was to save on Realtor commission. They thought that by representing themselves and just offering 3% to a buyer's agent, they'd save over $10k at a sales price of $340k. They were doing themselves a disservice though. I explained that if I were to list their home on the MLS for $380k and get it sold, even at a 6% commission rate they would end up netting $27,000 more than they would have with the deal that just fell through.

I was confident that I could get it sold for that price. Even though the property needed quite a bit of updating, it was an awesome investment. My confidence must've shown because they signed the listing paperwork. I was in for a little bit of an uphill battle though. The market was still frozen from Covid. No one was making any moves. All of our other prospects were pumping the breaks to see how this all played out. The first nightly rental property that we had just gotten up and running a few months prior (and that we were still trying to pay down the credit cards on) had ALL of its bookings for the foreseeable future canceled and the calendar blocked off after the state of Arkansas banned vacation rentals at the beginning of the pandemic. To top it all off, we had just purchased a fixer-upper with our good friends and partners that needed to be remodeled ASAP. We were feeling a little bit of pressure. Oh, did I mention Shae was pregnant with baby number three Jack Ryan?

I had to get this property to shine and get it sold. The seller lived hours away, and it hadn't been used much in years. It needed a deep cleaning and some maintenance. So we took care of it. The carpets got shampooed. The entire house was cleaned. We rearranged furniture and staged the rooms as best we could with tastefully chosen decor (from Dollar General) and took down the dated and broken blinds to let in the light and showcase the amazing lake views from almost every room. I loaded up my trailer and went to work. We brought furniture from our house over to stage on the empty deck. We bought a new rug to use that really tied the room together. I brought my mower over every other week or so along with a leaf blower and a string trimmer. I came over with my ladder and cleaned the overflowing gutters, patched up loose siding and sprayed the wasp nests that were accumulating. The deck was covered in oak pollen and the exterior needed to be cleaned up, so I brought over my pressure washer.

After a couple of months, the air of uncertainty in our part of the world started to subside. We received an offer on the property and got it under contract. Finally, there was a light at the end of the tunnel for this deal. The original buyer had been very thorough with his inspections and uncovered several issues that needed to be addressed while he was under contract. The seller already had it taken care of and the new buyer was content with the results of the first inspection and seeing the results of the repairs. Looked like smooth sailing once again.

Late the night before we were scheduled to close, I got a call from the agent representing the buyer. He also lived out of state and had asked her to do the final walk-through for him. She was standing in the basement telling me that it had flooded and the polished concrete floor was covered in mud.

One of the repairs that had been made after the inspections were done was to replace a cracked portion of the main sewer line where it went out of the basement. The seal around the pipe where it went through the concrete foundation wall of the house hadn't been properly installed and the heavy rain we received earlier that day sent a healthy supply of mud and water into the basement. We were scheduled to close in just over sixteen hours. So I went back to work. I came over with a mop, a bucket, a shop vac and every beach towel I could find. It took hours to get it cleaned up but that basement floor shined when I left. First thing the next morning I got the plumber who did the repair to come out with a backhoe and dig up the side of the house where he replaced the sewer main. He got the foundation seal installed that had been overlooked when they did the repair and I sent pictures of everything to the buyer's agent. The deal was saved, the seller got paid and the buyer was happy with his new lake house.

Starting out as new agents, Shae and I never hid the fact that we were inexperienced, but our confidence and resourcefulness put our clients at ease. Not only did they start to refer business to us every chance they got, but they also went out of their way to recommend us on social media sites. While many in our industry pay for lead generation services to find clients, we quickly found ourselves in a position where nearly 100% of our business was coming from repeat clients, word of mouth and Facebook referrals. Our reputation was a result of simply exceeding clients' expectations and I think a few other personality traits.

Practice What You Preach

Our real estate market is popular for investing in vacation rentals, also known as short term rentals (STRs) or Airbnb. We would get clients wanting to invest in them and frankly, we felt like deer in headlights— very intrigued deer though. While Branson, Missouri and the surrounding towns have restrictions on where you can do STR, we realized that since our house was just over the state line in Arkansas (only twenty minutes from Branson and two minutes from Table Rock Lake), we could turn it into a vacation rental. It was a cute A-frame with a view, so we felt it would do really well. We managed to get our friends to invest in our idea by partnering on the purchase of property up the road that we could move into and give this STR idea a try.

It worked. Our little yellow A-frame (The Crystal Cabin) turned out to be one of the most successful three-bedroom vacation rentals in our market. We were hands-on, from the renovation to the furnishing/set up, cleaning and management. Now when we would get an investor lead, we could speak from experience and advise them with confidence.

Bring Value

There's a balance between being an annoying salesperson or a needy business owner and being a professional that is well-known in the community. We created a Facebook group for our vacation rental. However, we didn't name it The Crystal Cabin, and we didn't constantly post trying to get people to rent it. Instead, we called our group Ozark Mountain Vacations and encouraged people to post pictures from their vacations, look for recommendations on fun things to do or just brag about the area in general. This made the group lively. People appreciated the space and they recognized who created it even though we weren't constantly advertising ourselves or our services. We were marketing to our target demographic without directly asking for their business.

We also created a Facebook group called Ozark STR Masterminds. We wanted to create a space for vacation rental owners to ask questions, seek advice, ask for feedback on their listings, vent and seek recommendations. Throughout our years in real estate and construction, we have developed an extensive network of contacts who we have come to know and have done business with personally. Rather than keep this list to ourselves and reserve it for just our clients, we've made it accessible in the documents section of the group. We share it publicly and encourage others to share recommendations and add to the list. We do post about our projects because they are cool and interesting, but we never end a post with "call us now if you want to buy or sell.. Blah blah blah" because no one likes that. It's annoying. The vendors on the list appreciate the recommendations and they, in return, send us referrals too. In contributing to the needs of our target market, even when we do not directly benefit, we end up benefiting twofold.

What do I do for a living?

I've had a lot of titles: restaurant manager, fireman, builder, Realtor, cleaner, broker... I provide spaces for families to create memorable vacations. I help real estate investors build their portfolios to develop multiple streams of income and build for retirement. I look at raw land and think of fun ways to develop it to improve the community and create jobs. I try (hopefully with more success than failures) to be the best husband, father, neighbor and Christian that I can be.

ABOUT RYAN DUFFY

Ryan Duffy is a real estate broker, home builder and property manager specializing in STR properties near Branson, Missouri. Following a series of back injuries sustained during his career as a Chicago Firefighter, Ryan (along with his incredibly talented and beautiful wife Shae) decided to give up city life in pursuit of star-filled skies, lake life and a quieter country setting to raise his family. His firm Duffy Homes Realty assists clients in the sale and acquisition of investment properties and offers guidance on the development of their land. In the fall of 2019, Ryan and Shae founded Ozark Mountain Vacations, which has grown into a collection of short term rental properties and five-star management in Omaha, Arkansas, near Table Rock Lake. While most Branson area accommodations are crowded into large condo or resort settings, Ozark Mountain Vacations breaks the mold by offering individual single-family homes on larger lots with private amenities. This enables guests to reconnect with nature and each other while still being just a short drive from major area attractions. Through their construction business Duffy Homes LLC, Ryan and Shae are creating purpose-built developments focused on preserving the look, feel and values that drew them to the Ozarks. The Duffys pride themselves on supporting others in their investment journey and emphasize the transformational nature of smart real estate investment for individual families and communities as a whole.

Website: www.DuffyHomesLLC.com

15 KATRINA MARTIN

Short-Term Rental Hosts have several tax breaks you should be taking advantage of

B ut before we jump into that, let me tell you a little about myself and how I'm qualified to share this information with you.

I'm Katrina L. Martin, an Enrolled Agent (EA) having earned the privilege of representing taxpayers before the Internal Revenue Service, which is the highest licensing credential the IRS awards.

I'm also an Air Force Veteran and Certified Tax Coach who specializes in working with Short-Term Rental Host and Investors looking to pay the least amount in taxes legally possible. I'm affectionately known as the "Tax Whisperer" because of my strategic tax knowledge and tax law expertise.

I have over twenty years Tax Advisory experience; I'm the CEO and founder of Wow Tax & Advisory Service based in Michigan. Through my tax planning program, I help Short-Term Rental hosts and owners save thousands of dollars in taxes, build a solid business foundation, and increase overall profits.

I provide practical tips from my background in advertising and vast tax experience. My goal is to guide you in better understanding how to optimize your tax savings.

So, now that you know a little about me, let's review my top tax recommendations for rental hosts and owners... let's go!

1. Depreciation (This is King.)

The IRS has four simple requirements to determine if you're eligible to take advantage of depreciation as a tax deduction:

1. You own the property,
2. You make money off your property by renting it out,
3. Improvements to the property (such as the actual house you are renting) have a finite and determinable life cycle. Their value can depreciate over time due to natural wear and tear,
4. The property improvement will last more than a year; thus, it will not be suitable or temporary housing.

Example: Normal residential rental depreciation is 27.5 years and commercial property depreciation is 39 years.

So, if you purchase a single-family rental property for $100,000, you would be able depreciate $3,636 each year for 27.5 years. ($100,000 / 27.5 = $3,636).

2. Cost Segregation

You can save money on taxes with cost segregation for your rental property. Although the idea of cost segregation was popularized in the real estate industry, the principles are equally applicable to the hotel and Short-Term Rental industry.

The fundamentals of cost segregation are the same, whether the investment is in real estate property or personal property. Cost segregation helps you accelerate your depreciation.

Example: Remember, standard residential rental depreciation is 27.5 years. With something like using BONUS depreciation, you can take 100% depreciation in 2022!

The one thing to keep in mind is how long you intend on keeping the property because of depreciation recapture.

"Depreciation recapture" refers to the Internal Revenue Service's (IRS) policy that an individual cannot claim a depreciation deduction for an asset (thereby reducing their income tax) and then sell it for a profit without "repaying the IRS" through income tax on that profit.

Having a long-term tax strategy is key because the sale of real estate may lead to a significant tax bill, especially if the asset has appreciated greatly or if it has had significant depreciation taken against it.

Having a tax strategy like a 1031 exchange allows you to avoid paying those capital gains taxes when you sell an investment property and reinvest the proceeds from the sale within certain time limits in a property or properties of like kind and equal or greater value. There are very specific rules that must be followed for a 1031 exchange, including the time frames the transaction takes place.

3. Furniture

While you can list your property on Airbnb or VRBO or other platforms as is, you'll likely get a lot more interest from potential renters or visitors if you renovate the interior. Consider how you would look for a place to stay while traveling; the lodgings that capture your attention are more likely to be booked.

As a result, many STR hosts find themselves purchasing furniture and décor to improve the appearance of their rental.

This is a legitimate business expense that you can deduct. Couches, chairs, tables, paintings, and accent items can all be deducted from your taxes. Just make sure you save all your receipts and invoices for tax purposes. Accounting systems are key!

I recommend using a system like QuickBooks Online or Xero, or at the least an Excel spreadsheet that tracks your business income and expenses. I can't stress enough how important it is to know your numbers.

4. Cleaning/Maintenance Fees

Another expense that Short-Term Rental owners need to consider is cleaning and maintenance.

As you probably already know, having a cleaning company come by after guest stays could cost several hundred dollars per week.

In fact, routine house maintenance may add up to hundreds (if not thousands) of dollars over a year. These cleaning and maintenance costs should also be considered company expenses.

Pro Tip: Consider building out your own cleaning staff to turn a hefty expense into a potential profit. Always think outside the box. Remember you're building your brand's reputation.

5. Marketing

Your home might be on a private island, complete with an infinity pool overlooking the sea. Yet, if travelers are unaware of its existence, it is will still be buried beneath all the other properties in the region.

It would be nice if you could just create it and have people come—but you have to sell it, just like any other business.

Expenses for marketing can quickly mount up! Everything, from hiring graphic designers, to developing ads to paying for paid social media advertising or reputation management; the cool thing is adverting is 100% tax-deductible.

Pro Tip: Whenever you're ready create your own hospitality website and CRM system to OWN your customer data at some point!

6. Home Office Deduction

This tax deduction is easy to ignore, mainly because it isn't directly related to the rental property. But if you do any property management or booking from home, it's one tax deduction you can undoubtedly take advantage.

A home office will qualify as a principal place of business if it is used exclusively and regularly for the administrative or management activities of your trade or business and if there is no other fixed location where you conduct a substantial portion of those activities.

"Exclusive" means the area can only be used for your trade or business. It does not have to be separated by any kind of permanent partition.

"Regular use" means more than occasional or incidental use and is determined from each taxpayer's facts and circumstances.

To determine what qualifies as a "principal place of business," consider the relative importance of the activities performed at each place where you conduct business and the amount of time spent at each place of business.

In the case of a separate structure not attached to your home, you may qualify for deductions related to it if it is used in connection with your trade or business.

In addition, a portion of costs such as utilities, homeowners' insurance, homeowners' association fees, security, cleaning, pest control, maintenance, mortgage interest, and property taxes can be deducted from business income if you qualify for a home office deduction. The portion is calculated by dividing the square footage of your office by the total square footage of your home.

7. Commissions and Fees

Airbnb withholds commissions and fees from bookings, which are tax-deductible. Airbnb will deduct about 20% of earnings from listings to cover backend expenses. How can vacation rental owners deduct these fees and commissions? Because your taxable income does not include the price that someone pays to stay at your property. You'll simply record the money you receive from Airbnb, which will already have the fees removed.

VRBO fees to owners are typically 8% per booking and are tax-deductible.

These expenses can really add up over time; don't leave tax-deductible expenses on the table.

8. Mortgage Interest, Insurance, and Taxes

You can deduct interest on the mortgage from your taxes if you have a mortgage on your rental home. And if your property has private mortgage insurance (PMI), you can generally deduct that as well.

And if you pay property taxes or property or casualty insurance, you can deduct those cost as well as home warranty insurance!

9. Other Indirect Expenses

If you hire a property manager to handle the day-to-day operations of your vacation Rental, that is tax-deductible.

Utility cost, subscription services for the property (ex: Netflix, Spotify etc.). Property management software, automation software, accounting software. Tax, accounting, and legal professional services are all tax deductible.

Pro Tip: Professional photography and staging fees are also tax-deductible expenses.

10. Travel Expenses

Travel expenses to perform maintenance or check-in on your properties are tax deductible.

Business owners are permitted to deduct reasonable costs for travel that is ordinary and necessary for your business.

Many business owners are reluctant to claim travel deductions for a variety of reasons, but there are legitimate steps you can take to combine deductible business travel with vacations.

Types of trips that usually qualify as ordinary and necessary business expenses fall into three different types of categories.

1. Travelling for new business. This includes traveling to scout locations, explore potential opportunities or acquire new investment property—it's all deductible business travel.
2. Travelling expenses to attend conferences and seminars are tax deductible and vacations can often be tacked onto these trips. Travel to and from the location is deductible, as well as lodging. However, non-business and non-conference days are not deductible.
3. Board meetings in resort locations can be deductible as long as the taxpayer can demonstrate a clear business purpose and a reason why the meeting can't be held at the business primary location.

Pro Tip: Travel costs for spouses and children who accompany someone on a business trip are typically not deductible. However, if they are involved in the business and have a business purpose for attending, the travel may be deductible.

Real Estate Tax Breaks Maximize Profits

Real Estate and Short-Term Rentals is a fantastic method to make money and business-related expenses can be deducted from the profits of operating your business. I can't leave out my rental arbitragers.

Rental Arbitrage

Many of the lucrative tax savings are geared toward the property owner(s) like depreciation and cost segregation.

However, most other tax advantages still apply for arbitragers. The rental arbitrage space is especially attractive as you don't have the liability of the property owner, but you can reap tons of profits and be very flexible on locations and the number of units you manage and host.

It's especially important for those following this business model to keep track of income and expenses, as you will not typically have property depreciation, mortgage interest, PMI, or property tax deductions.

However, you can write off the cost of rent you pay to the owner, out-of-pocket business expenses, home office expenses, travel, advertising, licensing, repairs and professional services fees.

I highly recommend running your numbers in advance of signing any contracts with property owners. Be knowledgeable about state and local rules as many states are changing rules for short-term rentals. With arbitrage, you can be fluid and go where the money resides.

Conclusion

There are over 400 tax strategies that can be implemented. It's ideal to have a tax plan customized for your specific goals and plans.

If you want to learn more, feel free to follow me on social platforms.

ABOUT KATRINA MARTIN

Katrina Martin EA is also an IRS Enrolled Agent who specializes in working with Short-Term Rental hosts and owners looking to pay the least amount in taxes legally possible, and the author of *Airbnb Tax Secrets: Optimize Your Short-Term Rental Business*, available on Amazon.

She is known as the "Tax Whisperer" because of her strategic tax knowledge and tax law expertise.

Katrina has over twenty years of Tax Advisory expertise and is the founder of Wow Tax and Advisory Service. Through her BNB Advisory programs, Katrina helps STR hosts and owners and will help guide them in better understanding how to optimize their tax savings.

Link: *www.facebook.com/katrina.l.martin*

16 RUBY SERVIN-ZAPATA AND JEROME ISAACS

Speaking things into existence. That is my mantra.

Every little girl has dreams, and every little girl gets asked what she wants to be when she grows up. I have wanted to be a costume designer for years! I loved working behind the scenes and making the actors beautiful with the costumes I designed or setting up their makeup for the character they were playing. But dreams often change... life changes. At sixteen, I became a wife and a mom. I knew my dreams would change; my priority would be my little girl's dreams, my future children's dreams. My goal in life was to make sure I would teach my children that everyone has a choice and that any choice one makes can change their path, but that one can still achieve big things. My son was born a year later, and my youngest three years after. I would then ask my children, "what do you want to be when you grow up?" throughout their childhood. My youngest two took longer, but their big sister knew exactly what she wanted to do. She loved the sea, dolphins, snorkeling...she was our mermaid. In 2007 my marketing career started without any college education; after two interviews, I was given a chance, which forever shaped my life.

I remember looking through the classifieds in the job section, I circled an ad, saying, "this will be my job...an advertising consultant"—I had no previous experience, but I knew it would be my job! My husband (now ex) then encouraged me to write up my resume that day and drop it off. I met the most amazing people during my years of employment. I spoke that job into existence. July 2, 2008, I told my next career into existence without even knowing. I was featured in the local newspaper as the Seguin Citizen and asked what aspirations I had in mind. I replied, "One of my goals is to be in the real estate industry by age twenty-eight" I have kept that article since then. The recession hit, and we lost everything. My family of five moved into my parent's home for the next three years while we rebuilt. My next big move in my career was also something I spoke into existence.

I would move on to be a co-blogger, opening the doors for my Marketing Director position in a publication a few years later. Sandra Greaney, the owner, would become one of my two mentors. In March of 2014, at twenty-seven years old, I received a phone call asking if I would be interested in interviewing for an assistant job with a top real estate agent. On St. Patty's Day of 2014, I entered the real estate industry one month shy of my 28th birthday, and I have never looked back. I proudly became an assistant to a top Realtor and team at Coldwell Banker D'Ann Harper Realtors. Chris became my mentor for the next five years; I grew as a person, mother, friend, team member, and entrepreneur. For the years to follow, we kept our top status within our company, our most significant year in 2016, earning the #2 team.

I would then utilize my marketing experience and develop a lead-generation tool to assist our team. Not only was I assisting with the daily real estate transactions, but I was also now handling our marketing and expanding our brand. I absolutely loved my job and going to work every day; the office culture was one to be envious of at that time. I met two significant people at that office, and I had no idea what was to come at that time. Without knowing, I was shaping the next phase in my real estate career. With age came wisdom and an understanding of why I loved what I did. My dream of being a costume designer didn't come true but working behind the scenes to allow the ones on the main stage to shine did come true. I learned I loved making my team shine with my talents and gifts. My children were now much older; they knew that momma worked hard for them. I would bring them to work consistently so they could see and understand what I did. They learned about sacrifices early on and how important quality time is since mom and dad were working opposite schedules. As an only child, my parents gave their 100% to their grandchildren. My mom, who the kids call Lela, helped us raise our children while her daughter was working towards her goals. I would be nothing without my parents. In early 2019, my assistant days were over; the year prior, I was silently battling one of the most challenging years in my life. My mother's world was shocked, and my life was going down the same path. I promised my family would not become a statistic and my children would not break. I would not falter with everything going against me. My children saved me during the darkest times in my life, and I went MIA for six months. I took that time to build up my mom, my children, my family, and myself. My health declined substantially, and I was losing myself. The hole was becoming too deep for me to get out of until one day... as I was sitting in bed, my son crawled up next to me and said, "Mommy, all I want is to see you smile again. You tell us not to quit; why are you?" It was a slap to my face, and I promised my children that day that I wasn't going to quit and that I would make them proud. My life was already being shaped when I walked into that Coldwell Banker office in 2014, and I had no idea.

Speaking things into existence. It would become a mantra.

Every little boy has dreams, and every little boy gets asked what he wants to be when he grows up. Little boys often want to be police officers, firefighters, and doctors but not this little boy. This little boy was uncertain of what he wanted to be. He was having too much fun being a little boy. Growing up in a little farm town in Pond Creek, Oklahoma, he was taught at a young age to farm, respect his elders, to work at a young age. His grandparents were a big influential part of his life, and he was the little boy that could do no wrong. He came from a well-established family. His great-grandad started investing in real estate while he was young and instilled the art of managing money while investing in growing wealth in his family. Granddad would start them young by purchasing items that can retain or increase value. This little boy started buying baseball cards and reselling them or trading them. This little boy knew well that whatever he did in life would back date from what he was taught when he was young. Unfortunately, tragedy struck his family at a young age, and his trajectory forever changed. With his father's unexpected passing, his family had to move away, and his mom would be the sole provider for the family. As with any loss, this took a toll on the family, and both his brother and his mom would move several times until one day, they landed in Seguin, TX, at the age of sixteen.

Life was challenging in a new state, let alone a new town that was quite different than what he was used to. His mom would work tirelessly alongside his oldest brother. He had challenges like any teenage boy, but he knew he was made for something bigger. This little boy, now seventeen, knew what he wanted to do. He loved playing the guitar and wanted to pursue music therapy. He applied to Berkley and was surprised when he was accepted. His mom has kept the newspaper clipping with the announcement. At that time, he was one of the first Seguin High School students to hold that accolade, but it soon became unreachable due to financing, and that dream was just that, a dream. After graduation, he joined a rock band and toured for a while before tragedy hit again. The unexpected death of his older brother shook the family once again.

Not understanding why things happened, he was now the head of the household. He worked several jobs with false promises until, one day, he obtained his bartending license and bartended at a local hotel. Not knowing that one day it would allow him to change his trajectory in life. After several years of bartending and living day by day, he built his regulars, which then became friends. One day, one of these regulars would start talking to him about how he could purchase real estate with little to no money. Days passed, months passed, and this regular started to talk more about how he was doing great investing and had left his nine-to-five. Intrigued, he researched and decided to obtain his real estate license. Little did he know that his life would never be the same. He kept his bartending job for several years while growing his real estate book of business. His regulars became his clients, and his clients became his friends. In less than three years, he became a top real estate agent and now had an extensive portfolio of investment properties, and he was living the dream. In 2008, he obtained his Brokers license for the state of Texas, not knowing that that year would be the start of another significant shift. The recession hit soon after, and people were losing their jobs, so his only option for his portfolio was to liquidate. Between 2008 and 2010 he understood the investor's mentality. While the recession was creating a max exodus of Realtors, he built his client base 100% on investors and became a top agent year after year. In 2010, he joined Coldwell Banker D'Ann Harper Realtors as a Broker Associate, and he continued to make moves in the investment world. Fast forward to 2014, at thirty-eight years old, not only was he successful but also the typical "bachelor." living his best life to the fullest without a care in the world. Earning many awards throughout his years and being known for his "cheerleader" attitude throughout the office. In 2018 he bought a condo on the Comal River that would be used as a Short-Term Rental (Airbnb/Vrbo). It would be a long process before anything could be generated since remodeling would take up to a year.

Fast forward five years to 2019...

Hi, this is Ruby and Jerome. We met in 2014 but never imagined what life had in store for us; it has been challenging and not without a fight. We joined forces in 2019 after many personal challenges but have conquered them as a unit. We learned and grew in ways we didn't know possible, but my son's wish of his mom smiling again came true. I found my gift again, and now I do what I love, and I get to show and teach others to do the same. I speak things into existence; we speak things into existence.

During the first six months, I learned that being a host was more challenging than I thought, especially with a property on the river. After 1.5 years of Jerome self-managing his condo, he was ready to throw the towel and call it quits. I asked him if I could help since I had helped a previous marketing client with hers. He agreed, and $6,000 later, I rebranded his condo, named her Las Palmas on the Comal, and finished setting her up. We were so green, but I researched, learned, and applied what I learned. We failed multiple times and at one time received a three-star, and I was crushed. It was now 2020, and I started receiving calls about managing other properties. After months of finessing the art of hospitality and creating a unique space, I asked Jerome, "Why don't we create an STR property management company." it wasn't time yet. We moved brokerages in town, and the real estate market was booming. I was asked to co-host properties and learned even more! 2020 COVID hit, and everyone's world stopped, not ours. Having a riverfront condo with private access to the river, we were 95% booked and grossed over $80,000. That same year, we bought ten acres in Terlingua (four-year plan) to build something unique that could generate a significant cash flow when complete. 2021 was a year of planning; we created a family dynamic like no other. My children, eighteen, sixteen and thirteen, and their dad, who I lovingly call my baby daddy, became our most prominent cheerleaders for what we were trying to build for our future. 2021 Stellar Investment Luxe Destinations, a vacation rental property management company, was born. We were now managing three properties, including a wedding venue. Our business was a five-year plan, and little did we know when I spoke, "let's get ten properties by 2022." that it would be the start of something we never imagined.

One of our biggest growing pains was finding reputable vendors such as cleaning crews, handymen, etc. For two years, we cleaned the properties ourselves, and it was wearing us down. We quickly obtained Airbnb Super Host that year. Summer of 2021, we had the opportunity to travel to Hawaii in May and then again in August. It became our goal to one day own property in Hawaii; my eldest's goal was to get accepted into the University of Hawaii to obtain her marine biology degree. We had a plan set for 2022—we are known to visualize our dreams and put in work to achieve them. 2022 without a doubt, changed our trajectory, and we had no idea what a crazy ride it would be. As I started growing our SILD brand in Facebook groups and networking events, I started getting noticed. I brought a different level of hospitality to our area. We were taking the hands-on approach, and we were getting tired. I needed to find a cleaner... in two months went through seven, and not one would stick. One morning I received a direct message from an out-of-state investor who was looking to purchase a short-term rental investment property in San Antonio, TX, and needed help with a knowledgeable Realtor. Jerome and I got on the phone with her and her husband, and we instantly clicked. In March, my health declined again, and I was hospitalized for more than a week and had massive surgery. Sometime during this time, I sent a screenshot of a property to the buyers, and the day I was released from the hospital, we went to do a virtual showing, put an offer and won! The buyers flew in for an inspection and had set up interviews with vendors. March 17 is a day we hold dear to our hearts. I asked for a cleaner and gained a partner, friend, and family that day. Mrs. Graham's Cleaning Ladies, Crystal and Dan, came to the interview. The rest is history. Our business increased by 800% in less than four months. We worked so hard and were thrown everything to break us, but it just made us stronger.

In May of 2022, my eldest received the news that she did not get accepted into the University of Hawaii. She was absolutely devasted and decided to move forward with her move to Angelo State University. She was more motivated than ever to work hard for a year and transfer. The day she walked the stage, our entire family was proud. The first in our family to attend college. My little girl was achieving her dream...she wasn't quitting.

In 2022, we expanded our SILD umbrella into divisions, Stellar Hospitality Interior Designs specializing in setting up STRs. It's essential to stand out and to make the space functional.

Stellar STR Marketing & Coaching, bringing my marketing knowledge and implementing strategies to achieve a greater occupancy rate.

Stellar Real Estate Investments launched an REIG to help facilitate the entrance into the STR space.

Jerome joined Keller Williams Heritage in New Braunfels, TX. He created *The STR-uctured Group,* an investment & STR acquisition company.

Launching in the Spring of 2023: Stellar STR Magazine, where we will showcase STRs, investors, and stories around the United States.

We were selected to be Airbnb Community Leaders in 2023 for our region.

The last three years didn't come easy, and we had growing pains like any other business, but we continued. Speaking things to existence has become our mantra. If you believe it, work hard, and allow yourself to be surrounded by the right circle, big things follow. I have been asking for a team, and as of January, we have a group of ten individuals that play a crucial role in our success. It's a team effort; no one is successful by themselves. My dream came true—I work behind the scenes and make spaces shine for others to enjoy.

Our dream came true, we have built a legacy for our family, and we get to teach others how to do the same.

And my daughter's dream came true—she will attend the University of Hawaii in the fall of 2023, and we will follow suit and build what we have made here.

Our family's story is just beginning; if Jerome or I had given up years ago, we would not be able to see that everything in our lives was leading us to where we are now. I beat all the statistics stacked against me; mom at sixteen, wife at sixteen, no college degree. My son, soon to graduate, aspires to be a lawyer and a pilot, and my youngest dreams of working in the pit at NASCAR.

Think it to existence.

Speak it to existence.

Write it into existence.

Work it into existence.

ABOUT RUBY SERVIN-ZAPATA AND JEROME ISAACS

Ruby Servin-Zapata and Jerome Isaacs are known to visualize a dream and take action. They joined forces in 2019, built a portfolio, and created six businesses catering to the Short-Term Rental space.

Ruby, a marketeer for eighteen years, dove into the real estate in 2014 in the pursuit of flexibility. *Stellar Investment Luxe Destinations* was founded in 2020 and experienced exceptional growth in the STR space. *Steller Hospitality Interior Design* was created to facilitate STR design.

Jerome has been a Texas Broker and Realtor since 2008. In 2022, he joined Keller Williams Heritage in New Braunfels, TX. He created *The STR-uctured Group,* an investment and STR acquisition company. He's also an NMLO in Texas, having helped many investors and homeowners. The two were selected to be Airbnb Community Leaders in 2023 for their region.

In 2022, *Stellar Real Estate Investments* launched a REIG to help facilitate the entrance into the STR space.

Website: www.STR-Haus.com
Email: Sildestinations@gmail.com
Facebook: www.facebook.com/ruby.servin

17   SHARON PACE

I'll never forget the physician saying, "Mr. Pace, it's broken again. You will need a heart valve replacement." Another specialist later tells us, "you also have liver cancer."

These two diagnoses came a few years after Larry's initial heart valve repair. We did not know the chain of events to follow, but we knew we had to fight it.

In October 2019, Larry went in for his second open heart surgery. I remember vividly the physicians and staff rolling him away and the tears flowing down my face as I stood alone in that waiting area of the hospital. The wait seemed forever, but I finally received the news: "the surgery went well, and the surgeon will be out soon." We made it through that surgery with a failing liver and recovered within a few weeks. Larry then returned to work in late 2019 after the heart surgery.

In January 2020, the appointments for treating liver cancer started. While treating cancer, the specialist also referred us to the Memorial Hermann Transplant Center as Larry had cancer and cirrhosis of the liver. A transplant was the only cure. To qualify for the transplant, the physicians had to combat cancer to keep it within the qualifying parameters. We must visit multiple physicians and go through a lengthy process to be on the transplant list. You know what came next, right? COVID, a world that shut down, and the transplant center put our appointments on hold.

In March 2020, Larry received the news that he would no longer have his job, as many others did that spring. Corporate America let us down for the second time in five years. The last five years have been hard financially, emotionally, and physically.

When the world shut down, I had more time to focus on how we could recover from the financial loss. I did and still do, have a full-time job as a healthcare administrator for Texas Children's Hospital, but I could work from home a couple of days a week at that time. It was during that time that I started researching real estate investing. I did what many other investors had done and went to YouTube and the internet for help. Scrolling social media one day, I found a seven-day mini-course for women. That course led me to find a coach who aligned with our goals and provided all the support, materials, and guidance needed to start a business. I can't tell you how valuable coaches are, and to this day, my first coach, Debbie Deberry, "The Flipstress ," gave me the initial confidence and tools needed to start my real estate journey. Debbie is still on the sidelines, cheering us on and coaching us through all the things that come with real estate investing and flipping houses. Debbie also has one of the top podcasts, which I have been featured on twice during the last two years. Take a listen to the "Flip Houses Like a Girl" podcast!

I started the course in the summer of 2020; we created our LLC, picked a business name, and purchased that first property to flip. The training we received gave us the confidence to attend local real estate events, talk to realtors and entrepreneurs, meet wholesalers and analyze real estate deals.

I spent my lunch hours and evenings working on tasks for the business. Larry had also gone through two rounds of treatments for cancer. He supported my endeavors and has been instrumental in our success. We both have individual strengths and know our boundaries (sometimes) ha-ha.

That first flip in Galveston, TX, taught us the process from start to finish. It also taught us what we wanted to do ourselves and what we did not want to do ourselves. This first flip sold precisely six months after the purchase, and we made our first big profit! Woohoo! Let's do that again we said!

While waiting on the close of that first flip to sell in April of 2021, we purchased our second property to flip. We had also been networking and attending events. By networking on social media and at local events, we found a General Contractor duo that handled everything from design to sourcing materials to all the sub-contractors. They were the perfect addition to our team as our lives consisted of doctor appointments, treatments, and a full-time healthcare job. We needed a more passive approach on this second flip as I needed to focus on finding more deals.

We formed a great friendship and relationship with our new GC team, and we still work with them today to create beautiful spaces for our guests! Yes, there have been some challenges but that is expected when you are buying coastal homes that were built in the 1930s.

As we were rehabbing the second flip, I continued deep diving into learning and analyzing deals in order to scale the business.

In May 2021, I reached out to a local coach for one-on-one guidance. As a result, I began weekly meetings with Misty at Her Mindset Matters. Through this additional one-to-one training, we quickly purchased three more properties.

Investing in myself and getting an education was vital. IT STILL IS!

As we were rehabbing the fifth property in July 2021 in Galveston, we decided to hold the property and give short-term rentals a try. To our surprise, the property did well even during the slower off-season. That property taught us a lot; we then knew we loved hospitality!

As we began to invest in short-term rentals, I joined Alex Sabio and Savannah Arroyo's Healthcare Professionals in Real Estate Facebook group and The Female Short-Term Rental Investors group led by Stacey St. John. I have learned so much from these two groups!

Right before we launched the first property on the short-term rental listing sites, we bought another property closer to the beach and in a convenient location central to everything on the island. When we purchased that cute little bungalow, we knew we would need to design it to stand out among the others. So we incorporated the home's historical features with the new sought-after designs of today's market and created a beautiful place for families to visit. Our houses did very well that summer, and we had some fantastic guests!

We then attended the STR Wealth Conference in Nashville in June 2021 after getting special permission from the transplant surgeon to travel. Once again, networking and education were vital to our success. We came back from that conference with new tools to be successful in our endeavors to run successful short-term rentals!

Once the off-season approached a sense of panic began to settle in. I took a leap of faith, listed both properties on Furnished Finders, and set the appropriate pricing. A few days later, I received a phone call, and we landed our first corporate lease for six months! Those guests are still with us and extended another three months.

In mid-October 2022, we unexpectedly received the call that Larry had a recipient's liver, and the transplant took place on October 14, 2022! This surgery was the toughest to recover from, but we are blessed and doing well today!

Our team was vital during this time as we had just purchased our seventh and current property, going through a major rehab. It is a 1937 Tudor-style two-bedroom and two-bath home with another two-bed, one-bath apartment behind the primary home. Both are now being renovated and set up as mid and short-term rentals.

So what does Reputation Driven means to us?

A good reputation is really just being a good human. Reputation is being trustworthy and providing good customer service. It's providing value to others and being of good service to everyone and in each relationship. Reputation is the driver of your success!

Reputation Driven is doing what you say, when you say you will. It's being present and loyal in all your relationships from personal to business. I put so much faith and trust in my team of contractors, lenders, cleaners, realtors, friends and family. My wish is for everyone to be successful! Are there tough days? There is! I still lean on the experts surrounding me to get us through those bumps and trust they follow through with the same respect and honesty. We figure stuff out together! We pivot when we need to; we always strive to leave people and places better than we found them!

It's crucial to build strong relationships and invest in those relationships, it is these connections that we need to be successful in the business and investing world. It is due to our networking and valuing of our relationships that we are so fortunate to have the great business partners we have today. We are successful because of our team and business partners.

We love to sit and talk to new as well as seasoned investors, and love learning from and helping each other. It is what drives us! We want to provide wealth and knowledge to those who came after us just like those before us did.

We often host small meetups at our properties for investors to come and ask questions. We love to help other real estate professionals and short term rental owners and hosts reach their goals to just start! I do not pretend to know it all, but I do strive to find the answers and be a support system. Larry and I have sat on panels at local events to share our knowledge of running short-term rentals and how to design them. We enjoy meeting people and giving back. We are still learning, but we take every chance to help others!

We have come to love old houses and watch them be transformed into beautiful homes for guests and families to enjoy in this beautiful Gulf Coast beach town. Moving forward, we want to continue mentoring others, scaling our personal portfolio and continue flipping and investing out of state in places we want to travel. The transplant may have slowed us down, but it did not keep us down. We will keep pursuing our dreams and hope to continue building relationships that will further us in our endeavors.

For you our readers, we encourage you to stay the course. Through life's challenges keep a sound mind, get around like-minded individuals that encourage you daily, and stay true to yourself and what you believe in. Educate yourself and network, network, network!

Sharon and Larry Pace

ABOUT SHARON PACE

Sharon Pace is a Healthcare Professional, Real Estate Investor and Short-Term Rental Owner. She has over thirty years of expertise in healthcare leadership. She, along with her husband, Larry, are real estate investors and short-term rental owners in Galveston, Texas, and are the owners of Pace Properties.

Sharon is part of two coaching and mentor programs that have allowed her to continue working full-time and begin a journey towards financial freedom. She has been featured on two occasions on the "Flip Houses Like a Girl" podcast where she analyzed recent flips to coach and mentor other investors. Larry and Sharon were recently featured panel guests at the Bay Area Realtors Networking Breakfast where they shared their most recent short term rental projects with local real estate agents, brokers and investors. Both Larry and Sharon spend a great amount of time networking and socializing at local real estate investor meetups where they are constantly growing their network and team.

Sharon and Larry's real estate investing journey began in early 2020 after they were presented with both a corporate layoff and a grim medical diagnosis that would require three years of treatments and surgeries. Sharon and Larry have been driven to succeed in their business by facing adversity and staying constantly focused on the end goal of financial freedom. Sharon and Larry enjoy spending time with other investors in the Houston area where they can learn from seasoned investors and provide value.

18 TONI BOER

We often hear that, to find our truest self, we must hit **rock bottom.** What does that even look like? To that, I'll say, "when you know, you know."

I was born in 1980 to a seventeen-year-old girl, and my dad was the twenty-something married guy next door. Yep, you read that right. That soon led to his first divorce.

I can't even imagine that scenario, but here I am, a product of it. They each tell different stories as to how that went down, why my dad left town and ended up married to someone else. As a seventeen-year-old girl, my mom could not care for me entirely, so my Nana did. She was my mom through my mom. If you ever believe that two souls are connected, that's how my Nana and I were. My entire life, she was my person. As I grew up, we lived and breathed antiques, old houses, Phil Donahue, Oprah, soap operas, Elvis, Conway Twitty, Bingo, Poker, Derby horses, going to catholic church, and her teaching me how to cook chicken and dumplings, homemade biscuits and the best sweet tea. I lived with her, my mom and my drunken grandfather until she divorced him when I was eleven, then she lived with my mom and I after the divorce until I was fifteen. She understood me in ways not even I understood myself. Even without words, she understood me. Her wisdom ran through me. That, in turn, left a distant relationship between my mom and I. It was never that I didn't love my mom; of course I do. I believe now as an adult in hindsight that we just didn't bond. Never much in common and never really understood one another. There was no comparison to match my Nana, and that grew resentment on both ends with my mom and I. It wasn't either of their fault. My mom was just a kid herself when she had me. My Nana did what she thought was the right thing—to love me without condition. One thing was always certain: I always felt loved by both.

At nine years old, I met my dad for the first time. Growing up, I heard only stories of him and knew that my Nana did not like him, while my mom glorified him and consistently said he was the love of her life. The visitation process started with him, his wife, and my half-brother, Clayton. At fifteen years old, I left the home I shared with my Nana, breaking her heart to go live with my dad. She couldn't stand the breath that came out of his body. For all good reasons, but I had to see for myself. The next few years I was distant from my mom and my Nana, witnessed him as an alcoholic, an abusive husband to my stepmom, and knew I needed to leave at first chance.

At seventeen years old, I met Simon. He lived in the neighborhood and was like no one I had ever known. If there was anyone who "looked" like Jesus, it was him. It came natural to him. He served me, never called me anything other than the sweetest names possible, protected me, and provided a safe place to land. At this time in my life, church wasn't a staple. My dad certainly never went. I only had gone with my Nana, but still never fully understood it.

Nineteen years old, Simon and I moved out, got an apartment and started life together. Barely making ends meet, we did it. Now, I was distant from my dad, stepmom and brother, while reconciling with my Nana and mother. I was balancing a full-time job and going to college for interior design and architectural computer-aided drafting (CAD). I loved school, had maybe one year left but had to quit to work more hours and thought I could come back to it sooner than later to finish. The love of old homes had grown deeper over the years. Simon and I got married in May 2000. It was a long road ahead, little did I know at nineteen. For a total of thirteen years, Simon and I were together, married eleven, had two beautiful children, and I absolutely loved being a mom. Most days I was very content. Everything I didn't get from my mom I knew I was going to give to my own children. They were what I lived for every single day, but I yearned for a life that I wanted to create. I still had this quiet fire burning inside of me for old houses, or really anything to do with houses. I didn't know what to do with the desire; I just knew it was always there. I would pray about my life and what I wanted and would hear this voice telling me my time would come, but not yet. I didn't know what that even meant. I just knew intuitively it would come.

When I was thirty-one, I didn't want to be married anymore. Plain and simple. I had been with Simon since I was seventeen, hadn't dated much and wanted to be free. Sad to think that I had that shallowness inside of me, but telling my story now, I wanted to be honest and transparent because my mess may be a message and inspiration to another.

So here I was getting a divorce from the father of my two children, basically with no reason other than I was selfish and thought the whole world was passing me by. I had stayed home with my children since they were born, and I wanted more. Simon was and still is a simple man. He was the most content person, never needed more than he had. Yet, I wanted more. He again showed me what it meant to "look like Jesus" without even knowing it. He forgave me for the divorce. He continued to be a wonderful father, and we created a lasting friendship that to this day remains strong. Grace by definition, and forever grateful for him.

Within months after the divorce, I found dating life. I met a man who was fun, daring, and exciting, all the things I hadn't seen before. Less than a year into the relationship, I was pregnant with my third child, his first. I thought the right thing for us to do was to get married, so that's what we did. Here I was again, a stay-at-home mom. On our wedding day, I was six months pregnant and at the reception watched my now drunk husband try to make out with another woman. The beginning of my rock bottom had begun.

Throughout my pregnancy, there was excessive verbal abuse so much so that the baby inside of me would go still for hours and I thought many times was dead inside of me. What had I done with my life? How was this happening to me? I was thirty-two years old and quickly falling apart. As the days passed by, the man I married showed me what being married to a functioning alcoholic looked like. I didn't tell anyone. I was embarrassed and ashamed. I wallowed in self-pity. I lost all of my self-worth and all of my confidence. Gone.

In early 2013, my sweet son was born, but the relationship with his father continued to worsen, becoming more toxic. All of the things I grew up seeing happen to my Nana by my drunken grandfather, then living with my own alcoholic father, and now here I was on the same hamster wheel. By 2014, we were hanging on by a shoestring not living together. He would come and go.

I remember telling a friend that while there was abuse, and while there was the drinking, he had never cheated on me. I would cry myself to sleep countless times, cover up bruises, and tell my kids to not say a word to anyone about what went on behind closed doors. Praying to God more than ever to give me a sign to leave or to stay. Looking back, God was practically beating me in the face with signs! I had three kids and no career to support them well if I did leave. Soon after I spoke to my friend, I found out cheating could be added to the list. Rock bottom had never been so real and the scariest experience in my life. Devastated and riddled with unbelief, I spent a few days at the doctor's office having every test known to man run on my bloodwork, and decided it was time to file for divorce. Lucky for me, my tests came back all clear.

I remember the day I laid on my driveway as he left the house. My kids were inside, and I laid there paralyzed. The cold concrete felt so good on my face. The world felt like it had caved in on me. No one outside of my home knew but my one friend. I was every emotion all in one. Mad, sad, angry, bitter, embarrassed, ashamed, worried, anxious, humiliated, you name it; I felt it.

Ten days before the divorce was final was the day I told my Nana and my mom. I didn't want to hear "I told you so." I didn't want to hear how I should have never left Simon. What I do know is when two women who have experienced the same, there's an unspoken bond. This added to my Nana and I's bond. One more thing we both understood, even without speaking it. I later learned it literally almost killed her in grief, knowing what I went through. She had been hospitalized for being so upset more than once.

My second divorce was final in 2015, and I had no other choice but to get myself together. These three kids needed me more now than ever. My daughter became the other half of me. While I worked, she stayed at home to babysit the boys. We had a system. I had no idea the effects that that marriage had on my two older children until time had passed. I could see their anxiety in things that they shouldn't have anxiety in. I could see that my young pre-teen daughter was discouraged with the idea of any new relationship that I might have. I had thought that by me leaving that toxic relationship it fixed everything. I was wrong. Damage was done not only to me, but to my children.

I was more cautious about dating. No one met my children. Any red flags that popped up, I was done at first sight without explanation. I began to wonder what my life had in store. I was no longer dependent on a spouse and by 2017, I bought a house of my own, on my own for me and my children! Happy dance! Although I was lonely, I made the best with my kids.

October 2017, I met a guy who would become my husband just six months later. Yep. You read that right, too. The prior three-and-a-half years being single, I was able to find myself and know my expectations.

Back to the "when you know, you know" phrase.

The whole world around me thought I was crazy, and probably a few thousand prayers went up on my behalf.

Andrew was a man who loved God. He took me to church. No one had done that before him. Church was always a fight in my last marriage, so I didn't go. It's not an excuse, just telling my truth. He introduced me to what being a Christian really looked like. We did small groups together and separately. My faith began to take root. This is where I learned that

God is always working up stream. He always goes before us to prepare the way.

Andrew was very career driven. Ambitious beyond anything I had ever experienced. He was stable in his life. He had two tiny children at the time, just two and three years old. He made me laugh; he provided even when it wasn't needed or asked. I wasn't looking for a handout or anyone to take care of me in a monetary sense. I wanted to be taken care of differently, and he completed that with ease. The even funnier part is that he is six years younger than I am. I was extremely nervous about that. I had three children. I was thirty-seven, and he was thirty-one at the time. I had zero interest in raising a grown man or dealing with any nonsense whatsoever. He heard my dreams. Not only did he hear them, he encouraged me to pursue them.

October 2018, I was baptized and fully gave my life to Christ. My sins were washed away, and there was a new life for me. This past year was crucial in knowing that God had gone before me to seriously prepare the way. I had no idea what was coming and could not have handled it had my life not been changed from knowing the Lord.

During all of this I found forgiveness for my ex-husband and my dad. We now have a relationship that shows the world exactly what grace and forgiveness look like. My ex-husband is a part of the team I have built and helps Andrew and I on renovating the homes we take on, and my dad and I have become really close. On occasion, my ex-husband attends church with us. Growth is a beautiful experience.

This same timeframe I began Southern Grace Home Designs. This allowed me to go back to the start of what I loved—interior design, staging homes for anyone preparing to sell their home. It started the renovation fire within me to create beautiful spaces, especially in old homes. Andrew is handy and knowledgeable in renovations, so that's a plus. He literally feeds my passion beyond words can describe. He and I together are a masterpiece. I have the vision, and he helps bring it to life. He surprised me in early 2019 with my real estate course. This little gesture was the beginning to my beginning.

In June 2019, I suddenly lost my Nana. Her home of almost thirty years landed in my hands. Six months of renovations, her house was sold to a beautiful new family.

By the end of 2019, I was a licensed real estate agent! I did something no one else could do for me. Now what?

I didn't have clients falling from the sky. That was discouraging. It took time and patience for me to figure out what was next with this license that didn't provide instant clientele. 2020 came and COVID hit. Kids were home from school, I was home schooling; Meanwhile, Andrew has always worked from home, but having kids home during the day made life look and feel a whole lot different. I wasn't focused on gaining clients or real estate necessarily. Life was happening in a pandemic. That was the focus. We had discussions about creating different streams of income outside of the regular w-2 tradition. Passive income was a phrase we wanted to explore. There was only one path in my mind, and that was real estate. We had recently gotten a bonus of Andrew's, and it was decided we would look for a home within an hour or so from where we lived that we could enjoy as a family and also rent as an Airbnb to earn extra money. My husband is a numbers guy, so any data we could find, he analyzed it. We didn't have any set town or city in mind. We simply looked in areas of the highly sought-after bourbon distilleries; what Kentucky is known for. We had no idea what was in store. We soon found a home and bought it. We poured a good amount of money into renovating it, down to the studs. It was our first STR after a long and hard six months. We listed it on a Tuesday and had our first guest that Friday!

The 127 Farmhouse was born and so was I. The success of this home continues to blow our minds.

From that point on, I lived and breathed everything short-term rental. Every piece of information I could find, I consumed. County ordinances I nearly have memorized, tourism directors and bourbon execs, I wanted to know them all, and for them to know me and what I stand for. Every person in the industry that I could get to, I talked to. Networking extensively in person and online. Without reinventing the wheel, I was creating a brand of my own in real estate. Clients were coming in. I was thrilled to have a career with houses serving people, literally matchmaking people to homes. The foundation was being poured. I had found my calling. That whisper I had heard for so long that told me it wasn't my time yet, was now setting me free and all I could think was I have a lot of time to make up for!

In 2021, I had set a goal for myself that I didn't tell anyone. That goal was to have three short-term rentals by the end of the year. The year went by fast and there wasn't a single house that I wanted to pursue. My goal seemed like a wash, and I thanked God I hadn't told anyone. Insert laugh here. Mid November came and BOOM! A house. We negotiated and went under contract. I was thrilled. It might not have met my goal of three, but I was ecstatic for a second STR. A week or so later, BOOM! Another house came into my sight. By the second week of December, I had closed on two properties, totaling my goal of three for the year's end! If that isn't proof of the man upstairs, I don't know what is.

The Kentucky BourBarn and The Tavern on the Trail were in the making and, like always, under renovation to create beautiful and unique spaces for guests to enjoy.

I've created a team of trusted contractors who are skilled in their trade. An abundance of patience was and is needed. I want to get to know people, their families, and their stories. I gather the information about where our strengths and weaknesses are and how we, as a team, can work best together. Renovating homes is a process, and working alongside each other is a task. My goal for my team is for them to love working with me and for me. My reputation is driven by that alone.

I have created social media pages for each property, including my personal page, State of Bourbon and Southern Grace Home Designs. The STR industry has given me several avenues of success. I want to be accessible to any client because my goal is always a long-lasting relationship. Each client is given my attention to fit their needs and get them to meeting their goals and best interests in my market that has so much to offer.

My passion is and always has been creating relationships, that followed with investor clients that I work with from all over the United States, has allowed me to create my niche in being the bourbon trail STR real estate lady. I provide a value and an abundance mindset that is hard to come by.

I show transparency in my work and the proven successes. There's a method to my madness that once the trust between myself and a client is established, I can provide results. Sharing with clients that my market isn't dependent on beaches, lakes, partial views, or any seasonal trend. My famous saying is "bourbon doesn't have a season, and it doesn't go out of style!"

2022 has allowed continued growth for me as a STR realtor and consultant. I now mentor and coach clients, provide STR property management, general contract renovations for my STR buyers and help new or seasoned investors discover Kentucky short-term rental success and tourism throughout the state. At forty-two years old, success doesn't have an age. Success doesn't have a barrier. If you have a dream, pursue it. Period.

ABOUT TONI BOER

Toni Boer is a licensed Kentucky real estate agent who specializes in short-term rentals, specifically in the Bourbon Trail area in Central Kentucky. Toni owns short-term rentals herself, manages properties for clients, mentors, and coaches and sources the best suitable homes for investors across the U.S., who want to invest in Kentucky.

Toni also has built a team of trusted contractors to fulfill another passion she has of renovating, restoring and bringing life back into old, somewhat dilapidated, eyesore homes in the communities she's involved in.

Engaging and educating clients of all things Kentucky has to offer is what drives Toni and has provided her successes. She loves sharing and helping new and seasoned investors in the market of her expertise. Toni offers a southern casual approach with her clients, sharing her own obstacles and being transparent of what the market holds.

Adding "author" to her resume is something she never dreamed of.

Toni is a mom of three, bonus mom of two more, wife to Andrew and was 37 when she started in her real estate journey. By sharing her story, she hopes to inspire others to go after their dream.

ABOUT AMA PUBLISHING

AMA Publishing is an international, award winning publishing company that champions the stories of entrepreneurs who are trailblazers, innovators, and instigators.

Forbes has said that, *"AMA Publishing is helping women reshape the future of publishing."*

We would love to help you tell your story. We have helped thousands of people become international, bestselling authors through our courses, multi-author books, and as solo authors.

Your story, it's ready to be told.

Website: *www.amapublishing.co*

Made in the USA
Coppell, TX
09 September 2023

21422640R00105